Brian Castle has been Bishop of Tonbridge since 2002. He was a parish priest in Southwark, Somerset and Northern Zambia and spent a period as visiting tutor at the World Council of Churches' Ecumenical Institute at Bossey, Geneva. Before moving to his present position he was Vice-Principal and Director of Pastoral Studies at Ripon College Cuddesdon, Oxford. Based on his experiences in Zambia, Dr Castle has undertaken research in the communication of theology across cultures. In addition to the publication of his research and a number of articles, he is the author of *Sing a New Song to the Lord* (Darton, Longman and Todd, 1994) and *Unofficial God? Voices from Beyond the Walls* (SPCK, 2004). He is married to Jane and has three children.

G000055421

RECONCILING ONE AND ALL

God's gift to the world

Brian Castle

First published in Great Britain in 2008

Society for Promoting Christian Knowledge
36 Causton Street
London SW1P 4ST

British Library Cataloguing-in-Publication Data
A catalogue record for this book is available from the British Library

ISBN 978–0–281–05970–6

1 3 5 7 9 10 8 6 4 2

Typeset by Graphicraft Ltd, Hong Kong
Printed in Great Britain by Ashford Colour Press

Produced on paper from sustainable forests

To Jane – a continual source of strength and encouragement – I dedicate this book with my love

Contents

Acknowledgements

One of the quaint practices of the Church of England is that the announcement of the appointment of their bishops is made on a day agreed between the church authorities and 10 Downing Street. I went to the reception for the announcement of my appointment as Bishop of Tonbridge and in the afternoon two hijacked commercial airliners were crashed into the World Trade Center in New York and a third into the Pentagon. Months before I had chosen the Coventry Cross of Nails, symbol of reconciliation, as the design for my pectoral cross. In an extraordinary and disturbing way, the theme of reconciliation chose me. I made it the subject for my study leave in 2005 and it has figured high in my life and ministry. Today reconciliation is an essential theme for world and Church – perhaps more so today than for a long time.

There are many people I would like to thank for enabling and being part of the journey that has brought forth this book. The Woods/Gumbel Fellowship enabled me to spend four stimulating weeks at Tantur, an ecumenical study centre on the border between Jerusalem and Bethlehem. I am grateful to the many people in Israel and Palestine who spoke to me about the often dangerous work they are doing to bring about reconciliation. I was amazed and humbled to meet so many unsung heroes, Israeli and Palestinian, Muslim, Jew, Christian and of no particular faith, working for reconciliation – we can never know how much we all owe them. I would also like to thank others who have spoken to me about their experiences of reconciliation, including staff at St Ethelburga's Centre for Reconciliation, Robin Eames, the former Archbishop of Armagh, and many whom I cannot name who have told of their personal journeys towards reconciliation.

A number of people have specifically assisted me in the writing of this book by their comments, suggestions, wisdom and insights. I would like to thank my SPCK editor Ruth McCurry and the many clergy and lay-people in the diocese of Rochester with whom I have shared some of the reflections of this book and who have provided me with much food for thought. I am especially grateful to Margaret Adams, Ian Ainsworth-Smith, Eithne Buchanan-Barrow, my daughter Sarah Castle, Graham Harvey, Mother Mary-John of West Malling Abbey and members of the Mission Theology Advisory Group for their conversations on the themes of this book. I would also like to thank Derek Carpenter, Paula Gooder and Philippa Smethurst, who come at the topic from different perspectives, for their detailed checking of the text and suggestions for amendments and additions. Derek Carpenter also gave his time and energy in organizing the reflection points and writing some of the prayers. My special thanks to my wife Jane, who has patiently read through the book and commented on its many revisions, and undoubtedly knows it as well as I do.

I acknowledge the insights of many commentators on the subject of this book and I have noted these in the bibliography; but I have been particularly influenced by the writings of Miroslav Volf, whose book *Exclusion and Embrace* has helped shape my thinking and writing on reconciliation.

Using this book

This book has been written to be used in a number of ways. At the end of each chapter there are reflection points both for individuals and for groups. The individual reflections are for the use of those reading the book on their own. Group reflections are for those wanting starting points for their discussion. Naturally, other questions may arise from discussion; if so, I suggest disregarding the questions at the end of each chapter. It may be that one member of a group could be delegated to initiate the discussions each week, summarizing what he or she has gleaned from the chapter. All group members should read through the introduction before their first meeting. Alternatively, an individual could read through the book either using or disregarding the reflection points at the end of each chapter.

Within the reflection points, reference is made to works of art (and a web site is provided) that illustrate the particular theme and could form a basis for silent reflection either at the beginning or end of each discussion. However, group members may wish to bring along their own artefacts, art or music that relate to the theme and enable further discussion and personal reflection.

Prayer is an important part of this book and journey. At the end of each chapter there is space for prayer. Please use it.

This book is filled with stories relating to reconciliation, and the common thread is the Christian story, which is a constant companion. I hope readers will add their own stories and experiences to those they encounter here.

Introduction

The human soul cries out for reconciliation. This God-given cry starts within and reverberates around all of creation. We constantly pray that warring factions within Iraq, Israel/Palestine and Afghanistan may find some form of reconciliation so that the people of those troubled areas may live and move forward in climates of peace and justice. Northern Ireland has shown that this is possible and that light can come out of darkness. Violence within our cities and disputes within our communities are reminders that reconciliation is often required closer to home. The Anglican Communion, buffeted with disputes about power, belonging and identity, is at the same time trying to find a way forward that will reconcile those in dispute. Reconciliation is often needed within and between churches. Again power, belonging and identity, frequently masquerading as theology, figure highly in church disputes, be it at local, regional or national level.

Reconciliation may be sought if friends fall out among themselves. There will be times when reconciliation will need to be negotiated within the family. Sometimes a wise family member can mediate a family dispute, but it is not uncommon for mediation to be sought outside the family circle. Probably the most difficult area for the work of reconciliation is inside ourselves – there are times in the life of every human being when there is a war within. St Paul speaks for many people when he articulates his own inner battle in the letter to the Romans:

> I do not understand my own actions. For I do not do what I want, but I do the very thing I hate. Now if I do what I do not want, I agree that the law is good. But in fact it is no longer I that do it, but sin that dwells within me. For I know that nothing good dwells within me, that is, in my flesh. I can will what is right, but I cannot do it. For I do not do the good I want, but the evil I do not want is what I do. Now if I do what I do not want, it is no longer I that do it, but sin that dwells within me. So I find it to be a law that when I want to do what is good, evil lies close at hand. For I delight in the law of God in my inmost

self, but I see in my members another law at war with the law of my mind, making me captive to the law of sin that dwells in my members. Wretched man that I am! Who will rescue me from this body of death? Thanks be to God through Jesus Christ our Lord!

(Romans 7.15–25)

In recent years it has become apparent that if the earth itself is to survive, there needs to be an ecological reconciliation in which there is a balance between the forces of consumption, regeneration and conservation.

Finally, reconciliation flows throughout all Scripture, finding its finest expression in the thinking and theology of St Paul. The apostle reminds his readers that Jesus Christ is the embodiment of reconciliation between God and humanity and that the cross is the focus of that reconciliation. For Christians, therefore, reconciliation enables a deepening of their relationship with God. This brings us back to the fact that the human soul cries out for reconciliation. The search for reconciliation is at the heart of faith and fundamental to humanity.

Areas needing reconciliation

I have identified six areas of reconciliation:

- Political: between and within nations.
- Social: between and within communities.
- Personal: between persons and within families.
- Intrapersonal: within a person.
- Ecological: between the energies that sustain and exhaust the earth.
- Theological: between God and humanity.

What will become apparent in exploring the issue of reconciliation is that all six of these areas are inextricably linked. If we are living in dispute with our neighbours, it will have something to do with dissonance within ourselves. If we are in dispute politically, it will be related to the way we conduct our lives as Christians. If we are in dispute as Christians it will be because we are not reconciled to God. Furthermore, the sixth area, reconciliation between God and humanity, is fundamental to all the others. It is the God-given cry that starts within and reverberates around all creation.

Features, not definitions, of reconciliation

But what do we mean by reconciliation? Is there not a danger that it is defined differently every time it is used? At its simplest, reconciliation refers to the desire to repair fractured relationships in order to move forward, but as we shall see, reconciliation is complex and, as the cross testifies, true reconciliation costly. There is a sense in which reconciliation is something celebrated before it is explained, and any discussion of it needs to focus on examples and the experience of those engaged in the process. It cannot simply be a fireside exercise. Accordingly, this book will use stories about reconciliation drawn from a number of contexts and encourage readers to reflect on their own experiences in order to create a living conversation. Reconciliation defies definition, and yet most people recognize it when they experience it: the following chapters will be organized around four features that must be taken into account for reconciliation to be achieved. The final chapter will draw together some threads that will help work towards an understanding of reconciliation rather than actually provide a definition. It will also identify some 'marks' of reconciliation – without these marks reconciliation cannot take place. Christian theology has a distinctive understanding of reconciliation, and it is the calling of the Church to reveal this as God's gift to the world. The four features – and there are more – essential to be taken into account when working for reconciliation are:

- Memory – or remembering
- Victimhood
- Forgiveness – not mercy
- The other

The following chapters will explore these four areas. First, some preliminary points need to be made about reconciliation.

Is reconciliation achievable?

Reconciliation is more a process than a fact. Robin Eames, the former Archbishop of Armagh, who worked tirelessly for reconciliation in

Northern Ireland, was visiting a school and was asked by one of the pupils, 'How do we know when reconciliation is achieved?' Probably we can never know. As human beings we cannot experience full reconciliation, but there can be brief experiences and glimpses of it. Celebrating reconciliation is giving thanks for a fresh form of relationship, usually achieved after great struggle, and making a statement about a new future; it is a recognition that an important milestone has been reached. But has full reconciliation been achieved? Is Northern Ireland a reconciled province? Is South Africa a reconciled country? Are human beings ever fully reconciled within themselves? Reconciliation describes the relationship that, however imperfectly, the questing Christian both has with God and, at the same time, would like to deepen: Christians are being reconciled with God but there is always a long way to go. Reconciliation is to be viewed from the perspective of eschatology, which means that complete reconciliation is a future goal that may not be achieved in this life – but working towards it will shape the way in which this life is lived.

Reconciliation for . . .

Reconciliation is not an end in itself but a means to an end. Reconciliation is in the service of a shared vision – reconciliation is always *for* something. For the Christian, reconciliation is the means to a fulfilled relationship with God. For ecologists, reconciliation is for the sustainability of the planet. When two nations stop fighting and work towards reconciliation, peace will be short-lived unless they agree a vision for the future. One party may be willing to opt for something less than what they want because, for a variety of reasons, they can no longer afford to continue the fight; but they will be biding their time until the right opportunity comes for them to rise up again. It is, of course, possible that one party may eventually be persuaded that the cause for which they were fighting is misguided or unjust, in which case they may work towards a shared vision. Whatever the situation, when working for reconciliation, there is always a vision, explicit or implicit, towards which reconciling parties are moving. The more the vision is recognized and accepted by all involved, the more likely that reconciliation is to be successful.

A psychotherapist, in describing her work with people, used an image that helps to understand the process of reconciliation and offers a means of working towards a vision of personal wholeness. She compared working with a person to working with an orchestra, many different instruments needing to be heard in order to make up the whole. Sometimes the process of reconciliation might involve inviting one 'player' or voice within the whole to play louder to allow the others to take notice of that individual voice. At other times, an individual player might be too dominant and need to be contained and encouraged to listen to the others. It is the skill of the facilitator/ conductor or psychotherapist to listen, encourage, understand what is being said, and contain the individual voices for the sake of the whole.

The psychotherapist's imagery is reminiscent of the work of the West-Eastern Divan orchestra created in 1999 by two artists and intellectuals. Daniel Barenboim, an Israeli, and Edward Said, a Palestinian, organized a workshop for young musicians from Israel and various Middle Eastern countries, with the aim of drawing together musical study and the sharing of knowledge between people from cultures that have traditionally been rivals. In the workshops, Israelis and Arabs communicate and express themselves through their music freely and openly while hearing the narrative of the other. The founders did not regard the formation of the orchestra as a political project but they did share a vision: first, there could not be a military solution to the Israeli–Palestinian conflict; second, the future of Israel and Palestine are inextricably linked and the Holy Land is a place for two peoples.

Not only is the orchestra a powerful experience for those playing in it, but it is also a profound statement of hope for those watching and listening to their concerts, which take place across the world.

Finding the time ripe for reconciliation

Conditions need to be right before the work of reconciliation is undertaken – it is necessary to wait for the 'kairos' moment, that is, until the time for reconciliation is ripe. Usually the process can only begin when those involved think it will work or when they reckon it is in their own interests. There is no point in working for reconciliation in the middle of battle; the fighting first needs to stop and there needs to be a just peace. There can be no reconciliation between a strong person and a weaker person: true reconciliation can only take place between equals. The South African Council of Churches said in 1968 that it was impossible to talk about reconciliation in South Africa while apartheid still existed. Partners need to recognize that they are equal before reconciliation can happen, if the risk of exploitation is to be avoided.

A need to change within

The most powerful movement for reconciliation comes from within and is motivated by love. The Israeli organization Rabbis for Human Rights (RHR) shows that it is possible to work for reconciliation from within, without rejecting the body that needs reconciling. RHR was established to fight for human rights of both Israelis and Palestinians, and is motivated by its love of Israel. In its fight for human rights, RHR is working for reconciliation. Religion is viewed as a bridge rather than a wall in this quest. RHR has a well-developed network to help in its objectives, such as educational programmes, a well-established legal department and a 'sisters for peace' programme to empower women. A number of its members have received international peace prizes for their work. One participant in an educational programme commented that it had influenced her Jewish identity in a way that allowed her to know that there are different ways of defining Jewishness and Judaism besides the way pursued by the state of Israel.

RHR's executive director, Rabbi Arik Ascherman, has frequently found himself in court because he has stood up for one group or another that has been treated unfairly by the state. For example, he and his fellow rabbis have often fought for the rights of badly treated Israelis *and* stood in front of bulldozers about to destroy Palestinian homes. In March 2005, Rabbi Ascherman was convicted of blocking bulldozers with his body. In a surprise twist, the prosecution recommended that the conviction be expunged in return for community service, on the grounds that it deemed the defendant to be an upstanding citizen – an indication that the Rabbi's deep dedication to Israel was recognized. Immediately after leaving the courtroom, the Rabbi laid the cornerstone of a Palestinian home that had been demolished.

In its fight for social and economic justice for Israelis, RHR supported Israelis adversely affected by what it describes as 'mean-spirited' attempts by the government and private sector to reintegrate unemployed people into the workforce. RHR provides legal assistance so that those intimidated by the legal system can appeal against cuts in their welfare benefits.

The importance of the desert

Those seeking reconciliation need to experience the desert, as the experience of Musalaha illustrates. Musalaha (Arabic for reconciliation) is an organization whose aim is to reconcile Israeli and Palestinian Christians. Its founder and director, Salim Munayer, is a Palestinian Christian who holds Israeli citizenship. Salim's grandfather had lived in Lydda (Lod) until the 1948 war, when the Israelis took over the village. The Palestinians were ordered out of the village, but Salim's grandfather and family, who were Christians, took refuge in the church. They remained in the village and were given Israeli–Palestinian nationality. Salim was then brought up in a Jewish school and learnt to speak Hebrew and understand Jewish ways. At school he was able to argue strongly for the rights of Palestinians. This was an ideal background from which a commitment to Israeli–Palestinian reconciliation could grow. When starting on the road to reconciliation, Salim tried, unsuccessfully, to draw Israeli and Palestinian Christians into dialogue with each other. He came to realize that the imbalance of political power between Palestinians and Israelis was a major obstacle in dialogue and reconciliation. In addition, at the age of five, both Palestinian and Israeli children have a clear view of who the enemy is, and in the last 15 years this view has moved to a demonization of the enemy. The situation has been exacerbated by religion, which has been used to support ethnic division. Salim decided to use the desert as a tool for reconciliation.

The desert encounter has become an important part of Musalaha's philosophy. Groups of young Palestinians and Israelis go out into the desert together, where they need to support and look out for each other in order to survive. In this hostile environment, the young people are forced to look on each other as fellow human beings – dehumanizing labels, such as potential terrorists and overbearing intruders, wilt in the rigours of the wilderness, and a transformation of understandings takes place. Church may be a place where reconciliation is discussed, but the desert is a place where reconciliation is experienced. In using the desert, Musalaha is creatively using a resource that, for the people of God, has always been a place of stripping, encounter with God, renewal and surprise.

In the desert, the people of Israel are fed, not by their own ability but by God's grace. They find the desert to be a place of unexpected resources when they are fed by manna from heaven or water from the rock; but when they decide to collect the resource and hoard it, then everything goes stale for them (Exodus 16—17.7). It is in the desert that renewal takes place when a new identity is gradually forged and the people of Israel are given the choice of life and prosperity or death and disaster (Deuteronomy 30.15). Even today, Jews look back to the desert as a formative time when, at the Feast of Tabernacles, they build tents as a commemoration of their time in the wilderness and escape from slavery.

For Christians too, the desert, a place of stripping, humility, uncertainty and humiliation, is also a place of focus, wonder and unexpected resources. John the Baptist, with his prophetic clarity and sharpness, was shaped by his desert experience (Mark 1.1–8). Jesus emerged from his time in the desert with a clear sense of the direction in which God was calling him (Mark 1.12–13). Today, Christians are called to stand alongside Jesus and experience the desert during the season of Lent, in order to be prepared for the stripping and surprises God brings during Holy Week and Easter. Every time a Christian goes on retreat, there is the opportunity to be open to the experience of the desert and to be renewed to view life from a different perspective. For all these reasons, the desert experience has to be part of the journey of reconciliation. Reconciliation cannot take place unless those involved are willing to lose everything that has kept them apart, such as hatred, prejudices and ill-formed ideas; it demands an openness to renewal and a willingness to put their trust and faith in something beyond themselves, which, for Christians, is the grace of God.

What is truth?

One needs to be aware of issues around the significance and use of the truth because it is not always the case that revealing the whole truth will lead to reconciliation. T. S. Eliot's play *Murder in the Cathedral* focuses this question when Archbishop Thomas Becket, who is aware that he will soon be killed, tries to comfort the women of Canterbury (the Chorus), who are terrified by a sense of foreboding that their beloved Archbishop is about to die. The Archbishop tells the women, 'Humankind cannot bear very much reality.' Revealing the whole truth all the time is not always appropriate. It is not right to tell a person with terminal illness the full details of what he or she is likely to suffer until (and unless) that person is ready to bear it. The amount of truth to be revealed has to be related to the context of the truth-telling and the purpose for which it needs to be revealed. So the amount revealed to the person with terminal illness depends upon that person's own desire for the truth and the way it will be handled. This is a difficult and sensitive area since it is too easy not to reveal the whole truth for the wrong reasons: no one person can make such grave decisions on their own. But so too is it possible to reveal the whole truth for the wrong reasons – if the truth is used cynically as a destructive weapon then it becomes a lie. The letter to the Ephesians reminds readers of the significance of the culture of truth-telling with the encouragement about 'speaking the truth in love' (4.15). In his book *Exclusion and Embrace*, Miroslav Volf recognizes the dilemma this brings when he writes:

> my assumption is that the struggle against deception, injustice and violence is indispensable. But how should the struggle take place? How should 'truth' and 'justice' be identified? Negatively, my argument is almost a Nietzschean one: there is far too much dishonesty in the single-minded search for truth, too much injustice in the uncompromising struggle for justice.[1]

Similarly, Rowan Williams, recognizing the ambivalence of the truth and the way in which it can be misused, writes:

> Since the Fall concealment is necessary and good in the sense that there is plenty in human thought, feeling and experience that should not be part of shared discourse. We are alienated, divided and corrupted; but to bring this into speech (and to assume we thereby tell a better or fuller truth) is to collude with sin.[2]

A thorough discussion of truth would take many volumes, but a relatively straightforward way of finding our way through it all is by willingness to engage with the truth and be changed by it. Jesus reminded his followers, 'If you continue in my word, you are truly my disciples; and you will know the truth, and the truth will make you free' (John 8.31–32). If this freedom is life-giving and helps and enables reconciliation, then there will have been a positive engagement with truth. If the truth is life-denying, is restricting and ultimately destructive, then there need to be serious questions about its use and understanding.

1

Memory . . . or remembering

––•◆•––

At the beginning of Desmond Tutu's book, *No Future without Forgiveness*, which narrates his experiences of chairing the Truth and Reconciliation Commission in South Africa, are the words, 'Those who cannot remember the past are condemned to repeat it.' These words were originally written by American philosopher George Santayana and can be found today on the entrance to a museum to commemorate what happened at Dachau, the former Nazi concentration camp near Nuremberg. Santayana's words and the places where they have been quoted are reminders of the power of memory. Our memory of the past affects the way we live in the present and the way we view the future. Memory functions like the rear-view mirror for a car driver. If, as we drive, we only look in the rear-view mirror, we will not go far forward before we crash. If we disregard the rear-view mirror, we may be able to keep going for quite a while, but there will be problems: what is behind will catch up with us, and there may be accidents as it tries to overtake in unexpected ways. When we are clear on the direction in which we want to travel, we can use the rear-view mirror so that we can be aware of and negotiate with what is behind and, in turn, move forward positively and confidently.

The past *affects* the present and future, but it does not always have to *shape* it – unless it is allowed to shape it! This chapter will explore memory and remembering and their significance for reconciliation. It will consider the relationship of memory to identity and the ways in which memories are captured in places. Reflecting on the potential for liberation and slavery in the way we remember, the chapter will then show the importance of forgetting or laying aside the past, before considering the role of remembering in the Judeo–Christian tradition.

Memory and identity

While memory is a powerful factor in shaping identity, it qualifies rather than defines who we are. Our identity does not depend upon our experiences of the past. A Christian's relationship with God defines his or her identity. If anything less than a relationship with God is allowed to define identity, then deep turmoil will follow when that 'less than God', be it a person or a cause, lets us down or is destroyed. When Ignatius of Loyola was asked whether he would be disappointed if the new religious society (the Jesuits), which he had spent so much of his time and energy in founding, were to collapse, he replied that he would spend some time praying about it and then not think about it any more. Ignatius did not view his identity as being based on him as founder of the Jesuits (even though others may have regarded him as such) but rather his identity was based on his relationship with God, which nobody could remove. It is the same with memory. Although memory of the past can have a powerful effect upon a person, it need not define a person's identity. Thus, the more we are defined by our relationship with God, the more the grip of the past on our identity is broken.

The corollary of this is raised by people suffering with dementia. If memory is a powerful factor in shaping identity, then what effect does loss of memory have on identity? The brilliant philosopher and novelist Iris Murdoch ended her days living with Alzheimer's disease. Her husband, John Bayley, who nursed her throughout her illness, writes, in a moving memoir, of an encounter with the spouse of a fellow sufferer:

> Memory may have wholly lost its mind function, but it retains some hidden principle of identification, even after the Alzheimer's has long taken hold. A woman I sometimes meet, whose husband is also an Alzheimer's sufferer, once invited me to share in a brisk exchange of experiences. 'Like being chained to a corpse, isn't it?' she remarked cheerfully. I hastened to agree with her in the same jocular spirit, feeling reluctant nonetheless to pursue that particular metaphor. 'Oh, a much loved corpse naturally' she amended, giving me a slightly roguish glance, suggesting I might be thankful to abandon in her presence the usual proprieties that went with our situation.
>
> But I was not at all thankful. I was repelled – I couldn't help it – by the suggestion that Iris's affliction could have anything in common

with that of this jolly woman's husband. She was a heroine no doubt, but let her be a heroine in her own style. How could our cases be compared? Iris was Iris.[1]

Memory and remembering

Returning to the question of memory in relation to reconciliation, there is an important distinction to be made between memory and remembering.

Memory is an intimation or impression of something that has happened in the past and is floating around within like a boat without an anchor. Memories can be vague and imprecise, yet also powerful. One person may enjoy going on holiday to the seaside each year. She may enjoy the sand, sun, fresh air and sea; this enjoyment may be deepened by warm memories of childhood seaside holidays. Another person may be reluctant to spend her holiday by the sea because her childhood memories are haunted by the occasion when a freak wave knocked her over, dragged her out and made her afraid that she would drown. Even though this may have happened many years before, revisiting such a place would not provide the rest and relaxation that a holiday is meant to provide because of the distant memory of her previous experience.

Remembering, on the other hand, brings the memories in front of us and tries to make sense of them, putting them into some kind of framework. Remembering is like putting photographs in an album – or organizing digital pictures on a computer! We look at the photographs and decide whether to put them in chronological or thematic order. On the one hand, pictures of birds, mountains, lakes and flowers may well be organized thematically, by species, location and genus. Perhaps the most spectacular pictures will be in a prominent position. On the other hand, it is likely that family pictures will be organized in chronological order and it is probable that pride of place will be given to those of whom we are particularly fond; conversely, those whom we do not regard so highly may receive scant – if any – representation. This is a reminder that not only is the organizing of the pictures an act of remembering, but so too is the *way* in which they are organized, our favourite memories receiving pride of place and our least favourite being relegated or even omitted – more will be said about this later. The opposite of *re*membering, in the sense of assembling memories in some kind of framework, is not forgetting but *dis*membering.

Places of memory and remembrance

Places can be invested with memories and remembrance. We have already seen that a simple seaside holiday will have important memories that can affect a person's decision-making. At the death of Diana, Princess of Wales, makeshift memorials sprang up around the country. The centre of London, especially around Hyde Park, became a huge garden of remembrance. As well as a mountain of flowers, there were other memorabilia, including pictures of Mother Theresa of Calcutta (who died the same week as Diana) and pictures of the Blessed Virgin Mary: in the eyes of many, Diana was identified with both these saintly women. Outside of London, 'wayside shrines' appeared. The foot of telegraph poles and a variety of other places, often strewn with flowers, spontaneously became sites of remembrance to Diana. Since that time, wayside shrines have proliferated, marking road deaths and local disasters.

Alongside these spontaneous places of remembrance, there are the formal places. Churches are sites of memory and remembrance. Through art and stained glass, architecture, word and sacrament, churches remember the Christian story as well as other events associated with local and national life. Their memorials and graves hold the stories of individuals and families. Indeed, in some parishes more people can be found in the churchyard on Saturdays, visiting and tending graves, than in church on Sundays. A church together with its churchyard holds a part of the communal memory, both living and dead, in its gathering up of the past and present.

But there are areas where powerful symbols of memory and remembrance compete with each other, and Jerusalem is prominent among them. Jerusalem is a place with competing mountains of memory on which people are building eschatological skyscrapers. To put it differently, Jerusalem is home to some of the holiest sites in the world, which nourish religious and political identities: they can be used creatively to feed distinctiveness and respect difference or they can be exploited for narrow purposes. Jerusalem continues to be a place of fierce political dispute between Israelis and Palestinians, and it holds the key to peace in the region. Some would say that Jerusalem is the heart of the world, and when the heart is sick then the whole body is affected.

In the centre of Jerusalem, in the old city, lies the Western Wall, formerly known as the Wailing Wall. The Western Wall formed the lower part of the platform supporting the Jewish Temple built by Herod the Great in the first century on Mount Moriah, where Abraham travelled to sacrifice his son Isaac. This support wall is all that remains of the Temple, which is the holiest place for Judaism. Jews travel to this spot from around the world, so that at the beginning of Sabbath and during the great festivals the huge plaza in front of the Western Wall throngs with worshippers and well-wishers. Israel and Jerusalem have been perceived in Jewish memories as the centre of the world of nations and, for a great number, the Temple is at the heart of it. Today, Israeli army officers take their oath of allegiance at the Western Wall.

Perched above the Western Wall, in an area known as Haram al-Sharif on the site of the Jewish Temple of Herod the Great, is the Dome of the Rock and Al Aqsa mosque. The Dome was constructed on the site where the Prophet Mohammed is said to have risen to heaven in his night journey. In a box next to the rock, hairs said to have come from the Prophet's beard are kept and shown once a year, during Ramadan. For Muslims, Jerusalem (which they also know as al-Quds) is the third holiest city in the world and the second most important place of pilgrimage after Mecca. Reflecting on the significance of Jerusalem, a twelfth-century Muslim wrote:

> Jerusalem is the residence of your father Abraham, the place of ascension of your prophet, the burial ground of the messengers and the place of the descent of revelations. It is in the land where men will be resurrected and it is the holy land, to which God has referred in his clear book. It is the farthest place of worship.[2]

A ten-minute walk away from this site, which bristles with powerful memories and remembrances both for Muslims and Jews, can be found another important hill that bristles with powerful memories for Christians: Golgotha, the place of the skull, where Jesus Christ was crucified. Over this spot, a great basilica, built in the fourth century by Helena, the mother of the Emperor Constantine, houses both the place of crucifixion and the tomb provided for Jesus by Joseph of Arimathea. For over a thousand years, Christian pilgrims have visited and fought over Jerusalem and the Church of the Resurrection (also known as the Church of the Holy Sepulchre), viewing it as the most important of all pilgrim sites. There is also a long history of fighting between Christians over this place, so much so that in the nineteenth century the ruling Ottomans created a prayer schedule and handed the keys of the church to two local Muslim families. Even today, the same families (Judeh and Nusseibeh) hold the keys to the holiest place in Christendom, opening its doors every morning and locking them every night.

As if having in one city these places of powerful memories and remembrances for three of the world's major religions were not enough, there is another mountain of memory in Jerusalem, competing in a similar way with the others. Mount Herzl lies a few kilometres west of the old city of Jerusalem and is a symbol of a more secular Israel in the midst of one of the holiest cities in the world. Theodore Herzl (1860–1904) is revered in Israel as the father of political Zionism and the founder of the modern state of Israel; his tomb is at the pinnacle of the mountain named after him. The tomb rests like an altar as the focus of a great space used for such gatherings as the Israeli Independence Day celebrations. Also on Mount Herzl are the graves of military and political heroes who followed in Herzl's steps and played a role in the founding and sustaining of the state of Israel. On the same mountain is Yad Vashem, the Holocaust Memorial, which graphically depicts the horrors and discrimination faced by Jews before and during the Second World War. Abraham Yehoshua, Professor of Literature at the Hebrew University in Jerusalem, reflects on the significance of Mount Herzl in the history of modern Israel over and against the religious symbolism of the Western Wall:

> The ceremonies around Memorial Day and Independence Day have once again revealed the vast difference between two sites that are formally utilized by the state of Israel – the Western Wall and Mount Herzl. The symbolic systems behind each of the places point to two almost contradictory options for the future . . . the opening ceremony for the Independence Day celebrations on Mount Herzl reveals to us a place full of grandeur, power and clear symbols of hope, a place that serves as the context for an impressive occasion that could be a source of pride for any nation. The site itself is at the summit of a mountain, wide open to the four winds. It dominates and is not dominated; it is

free; there are wide vistas in all directions . . . Herzl's grave, in the centre, is that of a unifying and beloved figure. The military cemetery to the north-east gives dignity; Yad Vashem to the south-west empha-sizes the moral justification of establishing the state, both in terms of the inner account of the nation and in terms of the account between us, the Arabs and the other nations of the world. This museum bal-ances Jewish history superbly between Exile and Restoration.[3]

With these powerful places of remembering so close to each other in the same city, it is not surprising that the Holy Land is so turbulent and unsettled.

The Western Wall, the Haram al-Sharif, the Church of the Resurrection and even Mount Herzl provide the heartbeat for Jews, Muslims and Christians across the world as well as for those who live locally. Identities, focused on these sites, have frequently been shaped in the cauldron of conflict over and against each other. Memory is shaped into remembering in a way that justifies the battles, conflicts and actions of the past and, in so doing, sets out a path for the future. We remember *for* a particular reason or *as a result of* a particular experience.

Yad Vashem, the Holocaust Memorial, is an example of this. The Yad Vashem complex contains a number of rooms that, through art, artefacts, documents and personal stories, chart the story of the Holocaust. It is a harrowing place to visit. There is the darkened Hall of Remembrance with its eternal flame and the names of 21 concen-tration camps etched into the marble floor. There is the Children's Memorial, a small round chamber in which a single candle flashes light around the walls as a voice reads out the names of the one-and-a-half million children who perished in the Holocaust. Then there is a large concrete hall, opened in 2005, where the visitor walks along gloomy corridors and is confronted by image after image of the horrific and inhuman treatment meted out to over six million Jews. The visitor emerges from this hall, drained and battered by the depths to which human beings can fall, onto a balcony that provides a bright, stunning panorama of Jerusalem. The message is clear: after all the suffering, here is the prize. Abraham Yehoshua described this above as 'the moral justification of establishing the state'. Palestinians, for equally potent political and religious reasons, embodied in stone as well as their national psyche and memory, also lay claim to Jerusalem as theirs, believing that it was unjustly snatched from them after 1948. In this situation, reconciliation becomes virtually impossible.

Liberation or slavery: remembering rightly

For reconciliation to be a possibility, let alone a reality, remembering on its own is not enough. It is important to organize the memories and remember in a way that will enable reconciliation: there is a need to remember rightly. If we do not remember rightly, there is the danger of being locked in the past and repeating the problems of the past. It is important to ask: for what purposes am I remembering – what am I gaining and what am I losing by the way that I remember? Are other people gaining and losing by the way I remember? What or whose need am I meeting when remembering in this way? Do I *need* to remember in this way? Am I liberated or enslaved by my memories?

Robin Eames tells of a woman he met in South Armagh who had lost her husband in the struggles of Northern Ireland and keeps his picture on the wall. When she looks at the picture, dragged down by the pain of his loss, her demeanour becomes sharp and haggard and she refers bitterly to the 'terrorists' who killed him. No way forward here. A past that is unredeemed affects the present; it becomes a means of excluding others from oneself and an opportunity of demonizing the other. Compare that to the way Nelson Mandela viewed the past on his release from prison in South Africa. The many years of incarceration could have resulted in his emerging a twisted and resentful man who plunged South Africa into a bitter and bloody conflict, but the way he remembered the past must be one of the miracles of the twentieth century. In his autobiography, *Long Walk to Freedom*, Mandela writes:

> It was during those long and lonely years that my hunger for the freedom of my own people became a hunger for the freedom of all people, white and black. I knew as well as I knew anything that the oppressor must be liberated just as surely as the oppressed. A man who takes away another man's freedom is a prisoner of hatred, he is locked behind the bars of prejudice and narrow-mindedness. I am not truly free if I am taking away someone else's freedom, just as surely as I am not free when my freedom is taken from me. The oppressed and the oppressor alike are robbed of their humanity. When I walked out

of prison, that was my mission, to liberate the oppressed and the oppressor both. Some say this has now been achieved. But I know that that is not the case. The truth is that we are not yet free; we have merely achieved the freedom to be free, the right not to be oppressed. We have not taken the final step of our journey, but the first step on a longer and more difficult road. For to be free is not merely to cast off one's chains, but to live in a way that respects and enhances the freedom of others. The true test of our devotion to freedom is just beginning.[4]

To put it starkly and simply in order to highlight the contrast, the way we handle memories and remembrance can make them either stepping stones or millstones. If they are the former, we are enabled to engage with the present and move into the future; if they are the latter, we are held back in the past.

If the past is used as a stepping stone, remembering rightly enables new (liberating) possibilities rather than merely repeating old (enslaving) patterns; in other words, a thorough engagement with the past can open future possibilities that would not be available if the past were neglected.

The book of Isaiah is a fine example of the past opening up future possibilities. Chapters 40—55 (known as Second Isaiah) were written about 540 BC, when the Israelites were languishing in exile in Babylon away from their beloved Jerusalem. Isaiah views the past as a power that continues to offer its gifts in the present and into the future. For Isaiah the life-giving past is dragged into the present when he draws on the example of Abraham and Sarah. He encourages the despairing exiles:

> Look to the rock from which you were hewn, and to the quarry from which you were dug. Look to Abraham your father and to Sarah who bore you; for he was but one when I called him, but I blessed him and made him many. (Isaiah 51.1b–2)

Isaiah reminds the exiles of Sarah's barrenness – until she became the mother of the nation:

> Sing, O barren one who did not bear; burst into song and shout, you who have not been in labour! For the children of the desolate woman will be more than the children of her that is married, says the LORD. Enlarge the site of your tent, and let the curtains of your habitations be stretched out; do not hold back; lengthen your cords and strengthen

your stakes. For you will spread out to the right and to the left, and your descendants will possess the nations and will settle the desolate towns. (54.1–3)

Isaiah is reminding the Israelites that God is able to transform what appears to be dead and without hope into an unimaginable future. The power from past memories is released to liberate into the future. Behind Isaiah's words is a warning that becoming too attached to the surrounding culture and forgetting God leads to a dependence on the whim of contemporary circumstances rather than on God's grace: gratitude recedes into the background along with memory.

Biblical scholar Walter Brueggemann has no doubt about the power of memory:

> The memory gives us freedom, flexibility and distance in relation to present definitions of reality and arrangements of power. Where the memory is muted or distorted, we will, unlike Sarah, trust only obvious possibilities . . . when the memory is forgotten, we will come to trust excessively in Babylonian modes of life as the only thinkable, possible modes. We will become docile, passive, submissive subjects of the empire, glad to have our life world contained in the imperial system which is the solution. Where memory is lost or nullified, we are left with only a range of present-tense systems to which excessive commitment is often made.[5]

The Lambeth Conference, a ten-yearly gathering of bishops across the Anglican Communion, called and presided over by the Archbishop of Canterbury, assembled in the summer of 2008. The Conference of 670 bishops met amid talk of schism and division: reconciliation was an unspoken item on the agenda. The Anglican Communion was struggling with issues around questions of authority and orthodoxy, brought to a head by Provinces in North America wanting formally to bless same-sex partnerships and marriages, and also by the consecration as bishop of a partnered homosexual man. Furthermore, some dioceses, arguing that such actions were contrary to the core of the Christian faith, were leaving North American Provinces to align themselves with Provinces which they claimed were maintaining an orthodox approach. For the same reason, some individual parishes were seeking to be overseen by bishops outside of North America.

These bitter disputes are currently tearing at the fabric of Anglican churches in North America, and there is the danger that they will spill over to other Provinces, including England. Concerned about the direction in which the Communion was moving, just over 200 bishops decided not to attend the Conference. As in all disputes of this nature, power, influence and finance are part of the explosive mixture.

Fortunately, these issues were not allowed to dominate the agenda of the Lambeth Conference. Evangelism, the Bible in mission, Anglican identity, social justice, ecumenism, the environment, relating to other faiths, the use and abuse of power, human sexuality and the Anglican Covenant were all given space at the Conference. What is most significant for the question of remembering rightly, however, is the context and atmosphere in which they were discussed. A deep refreshing of the roots of Anglicanism was a priority: following Isaiah, there was a looking to 'the rock from which you were hewn, and to the quarry from which you were dug' (Isaiah 51.1). The spiritual atmosphere of the Conference was set by a rich diet of daily worship and prayer, daily Bible study and daily indaba groups (a particular form of gathering traditionally used in parts of Africa), where the themes of the day were discussed. A three-day retreat preceded the Conference. Anglicanism shares worship, prayer and Bible study, as cornerstones of faith, with other Christian traditions, but other activities located the Conference in a particularly Anglican environment. Anglicanism links worship with mission, so that the one feeds and shapes the other. It also takes the world, the local context and the Christian tradition seriously, striving to relate the gospel to them so that the good news is proclaimed afresh in each generation in ways that can be both affirming and challenging. Indeed, the preacher at the opening service of the Conference said, 'God gives the Church an agenda out of the crises of the world.' However, there can be a cost to following this way. Sometimes the cost is small, though nonetheless hard, but at other times it can be martyrdom, and there are many Anglicans who have paid this ultimate price. The dioceses of the Anglican Communion also have a special relationship with the Archbishop of Canterbury, who is regarded as a focus of unity. These emphases were apparent throughout the Conference, but powerfully embodied in three events.

Firstly, at the opening service in the splendour and grandeur of Canterbury Cathedral, the Gospel procession was led by a group of Melanesians, who created an atmosphere of joy by dance and music, as they carried the Bible in a canoe bedecked with flowers to the place where the Gospel was to be read. Here was a visible statement that the good news had been embraced locally and was received with joy.

The second event took place part-way through the Conference when bishops and spouses marched through the centre of London in support of the Millennium Development Goals (MDGs). The MDGs set times by which measurable progress should be made. The goals were to end extreme poverty and hunger, make primary education available for all, bring about gender equality, achieve particular standards of child and maternal health, combat certain curable infectious diseases, especially HIV/AIDS, reach certain targets on environmental sustainability and work towards a global partnership. The timetable for implementing the MDGs was agreed by governments in 2000, but sadly, with the present rate of progress, they are far from being implemented in the time agreed. Bishops from the UK and the USA, whose governments have the power to influence the timetable for the goals, walked shoulder to shoulder with bishops from Africa, Asia and Oceania, whose people suffer and die because of the issues which the goals were established to alleviate. This is where the Anglican Communion is at its best, when the poor of the Global South and the rich of the Global North can stand together to challenge the governments which have power to remove the poor from their poverty. In his final address to the Conference, the Archbishop of Canterbury reminded the gathered bishops that 'to be with Jesus in unity, prayer and love, in intimacy with the Father, is at the same time to be with him among the rejected and disfigured'. In this way, unity and truth belong together. If the Anglican Communion can be passionate about holding together, probably shaped differently, it will be making an important statement to the world about moving forward together despite potentially destructive differences.

Finally, one of the most powerful moments of the Conference came in the final service at Canterbury Cathedral when the names of seven members of the Melanesian Brotherhood were placed on the altar of modern-day martyrs. The Melanesian Brotherhood is an order of Anglican brothers living a simple and prayerful life and known for their peace and reconciliation work throughout the South Pacific and beyond. In a violent ethnic conflict on the Solomon Islands, brothers placed their camp between the opposing sides in order to broker peace. Peace eventually came, but not before seven members were kidnapped and brutally murdered in 2003. They paid the ultimate price. The packed cathedral was completely silent, as brothers danced and sang, carrying the names to where they will always be held in honour.

The Lambeth Conference was organized in such a way that the bishops, who came from different lands and doctrinal positions, were able, together, to refresh the roots of their identity by remembering and creatively celebrating their shared past in present events. In this way, the power of past memories, celebrated in the present, can liberate into the future.

In a similar way, African slaves, torn from their homeland, tribes and customs, and forced into exile across the Atlantic to an alien land, found the roots of their liberation in remembering the past. More will be said about the experience of the slaves and the phenomenon of the African-American spirituals in the chapter on victimhood, but they are significant here because in the spirituals the slaves remembered the past by recalling God's liberating of the enslaved Israelites, with whom they identified. The Exodus was a common theme of liberation:

> When Israel was in Egypt's land,
> Let my people go;
> Oppressed so hard they could not stand,
> Let my people go.

> *Refrain*: Go down, Moses, way down in Egypt's land;
> Tell ole Pharaoh
> Let my people go.

> 'Thus saith the Lord,' bold Moses said,
> Let my people go;
> If not I'll smite your first-born dead,
> Let my people go.

> No more shall they in bondage toil,
> Let my people go;
> Let them come out with Egypt's spoil,
> Let my people go.

The Lord told Moses what to do,
Let my people go;
To lead the children of Israel thro'
Let my people go.

When they had reached the other shore,
Let my people go;
They sung a song of triumph o'er,
Let my people go.

So too, the way we remember the past on a personal level will shape the present and the future. It will liberate or enslave.

The need to 'forget'

The parable of the All-loving Father in St Luke's Gospel (a story often misleadingly known as the Prodigal Son – Luke 15.11–32) must rate as one of most moving and challenging parts of Scripture. The younger son leaves his father and older brother with his share of the family fortune, which he wastes and squanders. Having reached rock bottom, he decides to return home. The father, who would have been disappointed and even dishonoured by his son's departure and subsequent behaviour, welcomes his son back with open arms. The hurt and disappointment disappeared with the embrace of the son. The father's love and embrace meant that memories of the past were not a hindrance to a renewed relationship: he was willing to 'forget', to lay aside, not remember the past in order to forge a new relationship. Forgetting or laying aside the past is different from repressing or refusing to remember it out of fear or guilt. This area will be developed in the chapter on forgiveness, but it also needs consideration in this chapter on memory.

While in exile in Babylon, the Israelites reflected on the painful question of why they, God's chosen people, should be forsaken by God and left to languish far from their promised land. There came the realization that they had turned their backs on God and that the exile was the consequence of turning away. However, now that their eyes were open to what they had done wrong, God was not only willing to take them back into their beloved homeland but to 'forget' and lay aside his memory of the past:

24

> Do not remember the former things, or consider the things of old. I am about to do a new thing; now it springs forth, do you not perceive it? (Isaiah 43.18–19)

This is repeated and developed later in Isaiah:

> For I am about to create new heavens and a new earth; the former things shall not be remembered or come to mind. But be glad and rejoice for ever in what I am creating; for I am about to create Jerusalem as a joy, and its people a delight. I will rejoice in Jerusalem and delight in my people; no more shall the sound of weeping be heard in it, or the cry of distress. (65.17–19)

Another contemporary prophet, Jeremiah, speaks in similar vein:

> But this is the covenant that I will make with the house of Israel after those days, says the LORD: I will put my law within them, and I will write it on their hearts; and I will be their God, and they shall be my people. No longer shall they teach one another, or say to each other, 'Know the LORD', for they shall all know me, from the least of them to the greatest, says the LORD; for I will forgive their iniquity, and remember their sin no more. (Jeremiah 31.33–34)

God kept alive the memory of sin until repentance and transformation occurred and then he was willing to let the memory die so that a new relationship could be formed. Again, memory was being handled in the service of reconciliation – it was memory *for* reconciliation. In order to serve reconciliation and form a new relationship the prophet points to God's willingness to lay aside or forget: 'the former things shall not be remembered or come into mind' and 'I will remember their sin no more.' It needs to be stressed that this laying aside does not underestimate the wrong, it is not a repression and it is not an escape. Rather it takes seriously what has happened in the past and shows a willingness, when the time is ripe, to move into the future towards reconciliation. This can only happen when we have an active control of the memory and decide the shape of remembering which, in itself, is a sign that we control the memory rather than the memory controlling us.

The other side of this coin is that if we refuse or are unable to 'lay aside' the memory of a wrong perpetrated against us, even though the perpetrator has repented and been transformed, then the memory prevents us from being redeemed and we get stuck in the past. As long as the remembrance of the injustices of the past prevents a reconciled relationship, we will not be whole.

Remembering and faith

Christians have inherited from their Jewish brothers and sisters the emphasis on remembering as a fundamental part of faith. To be a Jew is to remember the Exodus; to be a Christian is to remember the death and resurrection of Jesus Christ. However, remembering for Christians is not only sitting around and telling stirring stories of the past, it is also relating and engaging with the story of Jesus Christ in such a way that compels Christians to enter into the story, be fed by it and allow their lives to be changed by it so that the world can be transformed. This powerful form of remembering takes place in celebration and worship, and its ultimate purpose is to reconcile the worshipper and the world to God through Jesus Christ.

At the heart of baptism is the remembering of and participating in the death and resurrection of Jesus Christ (Romans 6.3–5). The riches of baptism are expressed in a variety of images, such as cleansing from sin (1 Corinthians 6.11), new birth (John 3.5), reclothing in Christ (Ephesians 5.14), renewal by the Spirit (Titus 3.5), being liberated into a new humanity (1 Corinthians 12.13). Through baptism the believer is incorporated into the reality of Christ's world, in which the believer commits him or herself to try to view the world through Christ's eyes and live by Christ's rules. Viewing the world differently is the first step towards changing it. Archbishop Desmond Tutu never wearied of reminding Africans in apartheid-ridden South Africa that they were loved and special in the eyes of God, even if their political rulers treated them like the lowest of the low. They needed to see themselves from God's perspective rather than from that of their political rulers. Tutu argued that if God regarded them as special in his eyes, then it was only a matter of time before others recognized this reality. Once men and women came to view themselves as children of God and experience the reality of God's love, apartheid was doomed.

At the heart of the Eucharist is the remembering of the death and resurrection of Jesus Christ, which is renewed through the bread and wine. The Eucharist remembers in such a way that the fruits of Jesus Christ's action in the past become available today. When Jesus presided at the Last Supper on the night before he died, he gave his followers the bread and wine and said, 'Do this in remembrance of me.' Each time the Eucharist is celebrated, the circumstances of the Last Supper are recalled with the same words, 'Do this in remembrance of me.' Through the celebration of the Eucharist, the life of Jesus, surrounded by his death, resurrection, ascension and the sending of the Spirit, makes the fruits of what Jesus did available today, takes the worshipper more fully and more deeply into what reconciliation is about: the Eucharist is a means of reconciliation. Partaking of the Eucharist places the worshipper in a dynamic relationship with memory and hope. Memory needs hope to give it life and potential, and hope needs memory to launch it from lived experience. Christians try to live their lives somewhere in this heady mixture.

When Jews remember in their worship, the story of the Exodus provides them with a lens through which they are reminded that something positive can emerge from suffering. Similarly, when Christians remember and enact their remembering in the Eucharist, Jesus' death and resurrection provide a lens through which they can experience something unbelievably liberating emanating from suffering. For Jesus Christ, the very worst that the world could throw at him, death itself, became a means to a life previously unimagined. The hope that is deep in this experience has sustained Christians through suffering and martyrdom. But just as there is the need to remember rightly, so too there is the need to remember fully.

It is right and proper to remember, enlivened through the Eucharist, that God is with us in our pain and suffering. But it would be a distortion of what Christ did for humanity at the crucifixion if we did not, at the same time, remember that Christ also removed the guilt of the transgressors. 'Father, forgive them, for they know not what they do,' cried Jesus at the crucifixion. If we remember that God is with the sufferers and do not remember that God also wants to remove the guilt of those who inflict the suffering, then we are not remembering fully and we may be using the Eucharist as a means to justify the uses to which we put those memories. Half-remembering in this way can lead to a demonization of those who have wronged us or of those with whom we disagree. Demonization happens when we regard people as less than human and gain pleasure (sometimes a secret pleasure) from belittling and rejecting them. Jesus Christ has reconciled to God both the sufferer and those who have inflicted the suffering.

Remembering rightly and fully is a key ingredient for reconciliation. The miracle of the Eucharist is that it forms a reconciled community even out of enemies. It is important not to lose sight of the central fact that reconciliation is initiated by and comes from God, not from humanity. If we are working for reconciliation, then we are joining in the work of God. In the Eucharist we view each other as people reconciled to God and each other. The liturgical scholar A. Schmemann writes that in the Eucharist, 'we create the memory of each other, we identify each other as living in Christ and being united with each other in him'.[6]

For quiet, individual reflection

1 If you have not brought your own picture, look at Sassetta's picture of the Last Supper in silence for five minutes, <www.wga.hu/frames-e.html?/html/s/sassetta/eucharist/4lastsup.html>.

2 Describe a place of memory and remembering important to you.

3 Why is the place in which you choose to pray appropriate for you?

4 Picture an occasion when you have been able to 'lay aside' a memory for the sake of reconciliation.

For discussion in groups

1 If you have not brought your own picture, look at Sassetta's picture of the Last Supper in silence for five minutes, <www.wga.hu/frames-e.html?/html/s/sassetta/eucharist/4lastsup.html>.

2 Discuss the way that national victories and defeats are remembered.

3 What does the Eucharist mean to you?

4 Which places help you to pray best?

5 Consider places associated with memory locally, nationally and internationally, and try to assess and share their effect on you.

Prayer

Infinite God, whose years fail not and whose greatness is beyond telling, be with us whose remembering is limited, finite, selfish and frail: grant in your providence, that our memories may be enlightened by perception, tuned for the common good, and reflective of all that would build us up into the people you would have us be. And when, in the years of mist and shadow, our memory fails and we forget, give us the innate sense of knowing that you remember us, know us, and love us to the end.

Derek Carpenter

2

Victimhood . . . or not

———•◆•———

Jesus Christ was never a victim – at least not in the way victimhood is understood in the twenty-first century. Yet throughout the centuries the image of Jesus Christ as victim has dominated song, art and architecture. In a similar way, it is common to speak of people being victims when they are at the receiving end of mistreatment of some kind, but those being mistreated do not always accept victimhood. At a conference in Bethlehem, Palestine, on 'Boundaries, Borders and Peoples', a Palestinian speaker made it abundantly clear that although Palestinians experienced oppression from Israel, they should not be regarded as victims. By his protestations, he was making a distinction between being victimized and being a victim. If a person, or a people, accept the role of victim, they are being rendered powerless. The Palestinian speaker did not regard Palestinians as powerless. It may be that the initial trauma of being overwhelmed by another person, people or circumstance may for a while bring about complete powerlessness and victimhood, but this is not a place to dwell for too long.

This chapter is different from the other chapters. Whereas the other chapters discuss what needs to be included if reconciliation is achievable, this chapter will focus on the fact that victimhood needs to be taken into account if reconciliation is to be enabled. So powerful is the concept and experience of victimhood that, at some level or other, it always creeps into discussions of reconciliation. Victimhood is a topic that can create a great deal of emotion – there are some who, because of past traumas, are locked in the mode of a victim. Furthermore, it could be argued that victimhood is a state shared by everybody: regardless of how self-aware and liberated a person may be, all people are victims of some circumstance or other at some level in their lives. It is not our intention to increase the sense of guilt and blame nor to make people feel even more victimized, but victimhood needs to be taken into account and clarified because victimhood, as usually understood, undermines and prevents reconciliation.

First, the 'victimhood' of Jesus will be explored, followed by some observations on Jesus as a scapegoat. The distinction between victim and victimized will be in the background and there will be some examples that focus the difference. There will then be a discussion of the power of victimhood and the relationship between victim and perpetrator, followed by reflections on the way contemporary society handles victims and victimhood. The question at the heart of this chapter is the way in which victimhood impacts on reconciliation, and this will be visited time and again in what follows.

Jesus Christ the 'victim'

The Christian tradition is full of images of Jesus Christ as victim. When John the Baptist saw Jesus coming towards him he said, 'Here is the Lamb of God who takes away the sin of the world!' (John 1.29). According to St John's Gospel, Jesus' death fell on the day of the slaughtering of the Passover lambs, thereby sealing the link between the sacrificial victims and the death of Jesus. But while viewing Jesus as victim helps explain his completion and fulfilment of the Jewish rites of Passover, the transfer of victim status from animal to person causes difficulties and confusion. It is necessary to go back to discover the roots of Jesus' victimhood.

In trying to explain the significance of Jesus' life and death and its relationship to Judaism, some authors of the New Testament turned to the Jewish sacrificial system, where worshippers could atone for their sins by offering sacrifices. Mention has already been made of St John's allusions that Jesus' death is linked with the slaughter of the paschal lambs that were to be sacrificed, but it is the epistle to the Hebrews that develops and refines this comparison. At the climax of an explanation of the sacrificial system, the epistle identifies Jesus himself as the sacrificial victim:

> But as it is, he [Jesus] has appeared once for all at the end of the age
> to remove sin by the sacrifice of himself.   (Hebrews 9.26)

Jesus' self-offering superseded the offering of animals and put an end to the need for any more sacrifices as it was both superior and a once-for-all offering. This was how the crucifixion could be understood.

32

Jesus, instead of an animal, was the victim. But here the similarity between Jesus and the animal victim stops. The New Testament makes it clear that Jesus' death was self-giving. He had a choice about whether he should go to his death: he could have said 'no' and not walked the path that he took. In the Garden of Gethsemane Jesus struggles with what he is called to do, his reluctance to do it and his final agreement to take the path to the cross:

> Going a little farther, he threw himself on the ground and prayed that, if it were possible, the hour might pass from him. He said, 'Abba, Father, for you all things are possible; remove this cup from me; yet, not what I want, but what you want.'   (Mark 14.35–36)

St John's Gospel powerfully draws out the choice before Jesus (and it was this Gospel that made the link between Jesus' death and the slaughter of the paschal lambs):

> And I lay down my life for the sheep. I have other sheep that do not belong to this fold. I must bring them also, and they will listen to my voice. So there will be one flock, one shepherd. For this reason the Father loves me, because I lay down my life in order to take it up again. No one takes it from me, but I lay it down of my own accord. I have power to lay it down, and I have power to take it up again. I have received this command from my Father.   (John 10.15–17)

So, on the one hand, Jesus' victimhood was similar to that of an animal in the sense that he was regarded as a sacrificial victim, but on the other, it was totally different in that he had a choice.

Two further points need to be made to draw out this distinction. First, the Greek word used in the New Testament to refer to a sacrificial victim (*thusia*) only refers to animals, except in the instance quoted from Hebrews 9.26, where it refers to Jesus.[1] There is no word that means victims in the contemporary understanding of people who are completely powerless in the face of what is being done to them. Second, Jesus' 'victimhood' draws out the difference between an animal and a person. An animal has only its power to lose – it becomes totally powerless when it is captured and sacrificed; but whereas a person may be rendered physically powerless by an enemy by being captured, imprisoned or enslaved, a person need not be totally under the control of their captor. Human beings have a potential for otherness, a capacity to reach out beyond themselves, that is bound up by that part of a human being often described as the soul. In many ways, the soul does not belong only to us, but to God, and it is from the soul that human identity is derived: the enemy cannot gain control over it unless it is given to them. When it is handed over, a human being becomes a classic victim. There will be illustrations of this important distinction later in this chapter, but it is important to emphasize that although Jesus was victimized, he was never a victim. Indeed, it was when he was physically powerless, nailed to the cross, unable to move and breathing his last, that Jesus was, in reality, most powerful and the victory of Good Friday was won.

Jesus Christ the scapegoat

Often, the notion of Jesus' being a victim is confused with that of his being a scapegoat, though the two are close. The book of Leviticus gives an account of the Day of Atonement, when the people of Israel reconciled themselves to God by cleansing the sanctuary of impurities and themselves of sins. For the people of Israel, ritual and personal purity before God was – and continues to be – a key part of their religion. Part of the ceremony involved taking two goats, sacrificing one as a sin-offering and sending out the other into the wilderness, carrying upon its back the sins of the community:

> Aaron shall offer the bull as a sin-offering for himself, and shall make atonement for himself and for his house. He shall take the two goats and set them before the LORD at the entrance of the tent of meeting; and Aaron shall cast lots on the two goats, one lot for the LORD and the other lot for Azazel. Aaron shall present the goat on which the lot fell for the LORD, and offer it as a sin-offering; but the goat on which the lot fell for Azazel shall be presented alive before the LORD to make atonement over it, that it may be sent away into the wilderness to Azazel. (Leviticus 16.6–10)

Before the animal (the scapegoat) is sent into the wilderness, the high priest places both his hands on the head of the goat and confesses over it the transgressions of the people of Israel, which the animal carries away from the people to a remote land:

> When he has finished atoning for the holy place and the tent of meeting and the altar, he shall present the live goat. Then Aaron shall lay both his hands on the head of the goat, and confess over it all the

iniquities of the people of Israel, and all their transgressions, all their sins, putting them on the head of the goat, and sending it away into the wilderness by means of someone designated for the task. The goat shall bear on itself all their iniquities to a barren region; and the goat shall be set free in the wilderness.   (Leviticus 16.20–22)

The purpose of the ritual was to re-establish equilibrium within the community and with God. Indeed, the role of ritual was the reconciliation and reordering of both individuals and community, through sacrifice. After this ceremony, the people could be at one with themselves and God. Modern commentators argue that this particular ceremony had another important function: it was a mechanism for handling and dissipating violence and conflict brewing beneath the surface in the community (which every community has), which if not channelled ritually would break out in far more destructive and non-rational ways. René Girard is the most famous proponent of this school of thought. Some would be critical of the high profile he gives to violence and conflict in the dynamics of a healthy society, and he does not take sufficient account of the victory won on the cross by Jesus Christ. But he does provide significant insights into the way religion and culture function. Girard claims that every community has deep within it a rivalry that can break out into a violent form of scapegoating. Identifying and disposing of the scapegoat is a means of directing and controlling the rivalry and violence and restoring equilibrium and reconciliation within a community. Often, the scapegoat is seen as subversive of the communal order and a threat to the equilibrium of the society.

The story of Joseph is a classic example of scapegoating (Genesis 37). He was a threat to his elder brothers because he was a favourite of his father, Jacob, and he enraged them with his dreams, predicting that, contrary to what they believed should be the case, the older brothers would be bowing down to the youngest, Joseph. They therefore cast him out of their community. Examples of scapegoating today include anti-Semitism, racism and other forms of ethnic cleansing. Scapegoating is a non-rational activity that is liable to happen in every community, even (perhaps especially) those that regard themselves as rational and reasonable. The person or group being scapegoated is usually regarded as responsible for ills and disorders within the community. For example, immigrants would be seen as responsible for overloading the national health service or taking the houses that should be given to long-term residents of the country; people of other faiths would be targeted for being potential terrorists. The person who does not fit in with the community because he or she cannot or does not want to integrate with others may become the focus of suspicion if something goes wrong in the area. In such instances, the vigilante group, or the lynch mob, may not be far away.

In the light of this understanding of the scapegoat, it is possible to see Jesus Christ as a scapegoat. Although he is never identified as such in the New Testament, he is treated as one. He certainly was regarded as subversive of communal order in first-century Palestine and a threat to the well-being of society. It was Caiaphas who came closest to identifying Jesus as a scapegoat when he said:

> 'You know nothing at all! You do not understand that it is better for you to have one man die for the people than to have the whole nation destroyed.' He did not say this on his own, but being high priest that year he prophesied that Jesus was about to die for the nation, and not for the nation only, but to gather into one the dispersed children of God. So from that day on they planned to put him to death.
>
> (John 11.49–53)

The importance of viewing Jesus Christ as a scapegoat is that it balances viewing him as a victim. It cannot be overstated that Jesus was victimized but not a victim. Yet for centuries the victimhood of Jesus has been emphasized. Seventeenth-century Spanish artist Francisco de Zurbarán represented the way in which Jesus was frequently understood in his painting, *Agnus Dei*, which shows a bound lamb prepared for sacrifice.[2] Jesus' victim status is referred to in hymns such as, 'Alleluia, sing to Jesus', which concludes with the phrase 'thou on earth both Priest and Victim in the Eucharistic feast'. In 'Christ triumphant, ever reigning' are the words, 'Suffering servant, scorned, ill-treated, victim crucified',[3] and in the hymn 'Sing my tongue the glorious battle' comes 'Tell how Christ, the world's redeemer, as a victim won the day.' Many stained-glass windows equate Jesus being a victim with a passive obedience to what has befallen him. Nothing can be further from the truth. Victimhood understood as being completely in the thrall of one's victimizer was not Jesus' experience, is not a Christian virtue and will not enable reconciliation to take place.

Victimized but not victims

In the troubled Holy Land there are many temptations to accept the role of victimhood, which will hold up and even derail the much-needed work of reconciliation. One organization that has turned its face against this and positively uses trauma as a means of working towards reconciliation is the Parents' Circle, a group of Palestinians and Israelis brought together by the loss of close relatives as a result of the conflict. The Parents' Circle brings together men and women for support after the devastation of personal bereavement, and its members also speak to groups of their experiences and the way they want to bring about peace and reconciliation to prevent others suffering similar losses. When they speak, Palestinians and Israelis share the stage. Rami and Abed are members of the Parents' Circle and, at a meeting in the Old City in Jerusalem, they told their stories.

Rami, an Israeli IT consultant in Jerusalem, spoke of his grandfather, who was a survivor of the Holocaust, and then went on to tell of the disaster that struck his close family. Ten years ago, his teenage daughter went out with friends to a restaurant in town, when a suicide bomber struck. Knowing what had taken place, Rami ran in search of his daughter, hoping and praying that she would be safe. But the unthinkable had happened, and he spoke movingly of the moment he saw his daughter's lifeless body. He was traumatized by this experience and knew that he either had to seek revenge or work for peace. Rami threw his energies into the work of the Parents' Circle, encouraging the ending of the Israeli occupation of Palestine and the reaching of a mutually acceptable peace agreement through peaceful means.

Abed is a Palestinian doctor. He spoke of returning home to discover a crowd of people around his house. When he worked his way to the front of the crowd, he saw his father, who had been so badly battered by an Israeli extremist that his brain tissue had been exposed. If his father was to be saved, Abed had to act as a doctor rather than a son. Sadly, his father died as a result of his injuries. Abed too rose above a desire for revenge and joined the Parents' Circle. Both Rami and Abed speak from the authority of pain, and people listen. Members of the Parents' Circle are invited to schools, lead joint Israeli–Palestinian seminars, speak with politicians and organize residential projects to encourage Israelis and Palestinians to meet and speak with each other to dispel the myths of demonization of the other that have fed this conflict. By sharing their experiences and looking for hope, they aim to put cracks in the walls of falsehood and despair that divide Israelis and Palestinians. Israelis and Palestinians standing side by side, bereaved by each other's community, reflect the possibility of reconciliation. But the message of reconciliation they embody, while embraced in some places, is not welcomed everywhere.

Rami spoke of a group of bereaved parents, Israeli and Palestinian, being received with great honour in Palestine. They were driven through the streets with police escort, government ministers formed a guard of honour and they were treated with great dignity and respect. In contrast, there was an occasion when Rami spoke to another group, some of whom held extreme political views; after he had told his story and enunciated his hope for the future, one person commented that he should have been blown up with his daughter. Rami and Abed bravely refused to accept the role of victim – they refused to allow their lives to be dominated by the trauma inflicted by others. But for some they spoke to, leaving behind the role of the victim and working towards reconciliation was too costly because they had too much to lose.

Probably the time when many people are confronted most dramatically with the issue of victimhood is with serious and terminal illness. Such occasions elicit, at some level, the question, Why me? Why should this happen to me? Jesus asked a similar question when he was on the cross and cried out, 'My God, my God, why have you forsaken me?' (Mark 15.34). It is at this point that a decision will be made – consciously or sub-consciously – about how to respond to and handle the illness. The response will be influenced by the way that similar situations have been handled in the past, but it does not have to be dictated by the past unless the individual allows it. On these occasions we are stripped to the core of our beings and need to respond from the very depths of who we are.

The Psalms are a treasury in these instances. They teem with stories of people who have struggled in dismal circumstances, refuse to be victims, and turn to God for support. Psalm 84 (vv. 4–5) catches this spirit beautifully as it talks about possibilities in barrenness:

Blessed are those whose strength is in you,
in whose heart are the highways to Zion,

Who going through the barren valley find there a spring,
and the early rains will clothe it with blessing.

The writer in Psalm 61 (vv. 1–2) is aware that although suffering may be all-surrounding at present, that is not all of life, and a wider vision will prevent his soul being as overwhelmed as his body. He prays that he may be lifted above his trials:

Hear my crying, O God,
and listen to my prayer.

From the end of the earth I call to you with fainting heart;
O set me on the rock that is higher than I.

In Psalm 69 (vv. 1–4, 15–16), the Psalmist describes his agony in terms of drowning, and although there is disguised anger against God in these words, nevertheless it is a trust in God, against all the odds, that prevents the writer from moving from being victimized to being victim:

Save me, O God,
for the waters have come up, even to my neck.

I sink in deep mire where there is no foothold;
I have come into deep waters and the flood sweeps over me.

I have grown weary with crying; my throat is raw;
my eyes have failed from looking so long for my God.

Those who hate me without any cause
are more than the hairs of my head;

. . .

Answer me, O God, in the abundance of your mercy
and with your sure salvation.

Draw me out of the mire, that I sink not;
Let me be rescued from those who hate me and out of the deep
    waters.

In these examples, those in pain and distress stretch out beyond themselves, to God, to prevent themselves from being overwhelmed by what oppresses them. Their bodies may deteriorate, but there is something else, the soul, that contains the essence of who they are.

In September 2007, Jane Tomlinson died of cancer at the age of 43. Hers was a remarkable story in which she refused to accept victimhood under the most trying of circumstances. She had treatment for breast cancer in 1991 when she was 26 years old, but the disease returned in 2000 throughout her body and she was given 12 months to live. In the next six years, Jane completed a number of athletic challenges, raising £1.5 million for charity. She completed the London Marathon three times, the London triathlon twice, the New York marathon, and cycled across Europe, Africa and the USA. She did all of this while living with terminal cancer. She struggled to complete the ride across the USA because of the pain and sickness, but she was determined to do this, her last sporting exploit, before spending time with her family in the last year of her life. Delivering a eulogy at her funeral service, her husband, Mike, said that she was always accepting of her fate, praying not for a miracle cure but for peace. At the same service, her parish priest spoke of her 'indomitable spirit'.

This is an exceptional example of a courageous woman who embraced her humanity and refused to accept victimhood. But many other people, who will be known only to a few, are no less courageous in the ways they refuse to be made victims even in the middle of great tribulation.

There are times when a refusal to accept victimhood is revealed in less obvious and dramatic ways. Such a refusal is well encapsulated in the Ethiopian proverb, 'When the great lord passes, the wise peasant bows deeply and silently farts.' Although on the surface a group of people may appear to be totally subservient and accepting of the oppression that locates them in the role of the classic victim, their refusal to accept this role can be seen in quiet or hidden or even disguised ways. If a group of oppressed or overwhelmed people are to survive and maintain their humanity, they have to resort to subterfuge until the time comes when they are free to express their humanity without fear. Refusing to accept victimhood ranges from simple, almost accidental actions to sophisticated movements. Examples of the former are jokes against the powerful and taking the opportunity, when passing, to push into them 'by accident' harder than usual. An example of a sophisticated movement is to be seen in the development of the African-American spirituals, which have already been referred to in Chapter 1 to illustrate the significance of memory. For our purposes here, it is important to be reminded of the horror of this dark chapter in human history.

The circumstances in which those taken to be slaves were transported from their homes in Africa to their places of enslavement in Britain and the Americas, and the conditions under which they worked, were appalling. Ottobah Cugoano, enslaved on the plantations in Grenada, described his experience in these words:

> Being in this dreadful captivity and horrible slavery, without any hope of deliverance, for about eight or nine months, beholding the most dreadful scenes of misery and cruelty, and seeing my miserable companions often cruelly lashed, and, as it were, cut to pieces, for the most trifling faults; this made me often tremble and weep, but I escaped better than many of them. For eating a piece of sugar-cane, some were cruelly lashed, struck over the face, to knock their teeth out. Some of the stouter ones, I suppose, often reproved, and grown hardened and stupid with many cruel beatings and lashings, or perhaps faint and pressed with hunger and hard labour, were often committing trespasses of this kind, and when detected, they met with exemplary punishment. Some told me they had their teeth pulled out, to deter others, and to prevent them from eating any cane in future.[4]

Although the Plantation owners possessed the bodies of the slaves, they did not possess their souls. The spirituals they sang are evidence of an inner freedom. They are based on biblical stories, usually of liberation, which are applied directly to the slaves' situation. By singing the spirituals, the power of God that liberated the heroes of the Bible is drawn upon in order to liberate the slaves:

> My Lord delivered Daniel,
> My Lord delivered Daniel,
> My Lord delivered Daniel,
> Why can't He deliver me?

What is remarkable is the way the slaves used the religion of the slave master. Christianity was a slave master's religion; indeed, it frequently justified the inhuman action of the slave master. But by some incredible spiritual insight, the slaves took on the religion that the master had profaned in their midst, made it their own and transformed it from being a justification of slavery to becoming a means of liberation. For example, the prophet Jeremiah comes to a great depression in his life and cries out from the depth of his despair, 'Is there no balm in Gilead? Is there no physician there?' (8.22). Jeremiah utters this cry in the midst of his soul-searching when, stripped bare of everything, he is confronted with the core of his own faith. He is actually saying that there must be balm in Gilead. The slaves caught the mood of this dilemma because they had shared such an ordeal, and the result is a spiritual that actually answers Jeremiah's deep questioning from the depths of their own experience:

> There is a balm in Gilead,
> To make the spirit whole,
> There is a balm in Gilead,
> To heal the sin-sick soul.

Another example of the slaves' use of their master's religion to speak to their particular situation is illustrated in the spiritual, 'I got shoes'. In this the slaves not only show their refusal to accept victimhood by using faith as a means of liberation and vindication, they also show that the master is the one who is ultimately to be enslaved. Slaves would have heard their master talk of heaven, the reward of the righteous, and of hell, the abode of the unjust. Naturally the master would see himself as going to heaven. Yet the slave was also convinced that he or she would be going there. The slave reasoned that he was having his hell now, and when he dies he will be going to heaven. Conversely, the master was having his heaven now and when he dies, he will be going to hell. So when the slaves sang about shoes (which, as symbols of true wealth, they did not possess on earth) they believed that shoes would be waiting for them in heaven. The last two lines in the spiritual signify that their masters would not be going to heaven:

> I got shoes, you got shoes,
> All God's children got shoes.
> When we get to Heaven
> We're goin' to put on our shoes
> An' shout all over God's Heaven.
> Heaven! Heaven!
> But everybody talking 'bout Heaven
> Ain't going there.

The slaves may have been victimized but they were certainly not victims. Nowhere is this better illustrated than in the spiritual, 'Oh Freedom':

> Oh Freedom! Oh Freedom!
> Oh, Freedom, I love thee!
> And before I'll be a slave,
> I'll be buried in my grave,
> And go home to my Lord and be free.

Refusing to accept victimhood is a powerful political weapon. When the struggle against apartheid was at its height, Desmond Tutu was asked whether he feared for his life. Tutu replied that his enemies could kill his body, but they could not kill the real 'him' because that was in God's hands, and they could never kill the cause of justice for which he fought. Not even the most powerful weapons that can be mustered stand a chance against a person and a cause like that.

Another powerful tool in the hands of those who have been victimized is the willingness to initiate a process of reconciliation. If those in power begin the process against the will of those who have been victimized, then it will not succeed, because there has to be a level of equality between those seeking reconciliation. It was while he was in prison that Nelson Mandela began talks about reconciliation with the South African government. But it was on his terms.

In January 1985, the South African President, P. W. Botha, under international pressure and the threat of sanctions, wanted to have Mandela released from prison, provided Mandela rejected violence unconditionally as a political instrument. Botha extended this offer to all political prisoners. Mandela refused the offer because he was unwilling to be set free into a society that was the same as when he was arrested. He reasoned that to be true to himself and the cause of real freedom for all South Africans, he would be forced to resume the same activities for which he was arrested. Nevertheless, he thought that negotiation and not war was the way to a solution. In a powerful speech explaining his actions, which was read by his daughter to a rally of supporters in Soweto, he said:

> I cherish my own freedom dearly, but I care even more for your freedom . . . I cannot sell my birthright, nor am I prepared to sell the birthright of the people to be free . . .

What freedom am I being offered while the organization of the people remains banned? What freedom am I being offered when I may be arrested on a pass offence? What freedom am I being offered to live my life as a family with my dear wife who remains in punishment in Brandfort? What freedom am I being offered when I must ask for permission to live in an urban area? . . . What freedom am I being offered when my very South African citizenship is not respected?

Only free men can negotiate. Prisoners cannot enter into contracts . . . I cannot give any undertaking at a time when you, the people, are not free. Your freedom and mine cannot be separated. I will return.[5]

In 1985 it was discovered that Mandela needed surgery for an enlarged prostate gland. While recuperating in Volks Hospital in Cape Town, he was visited by the minister of justice, to whom Mandela had written, some time before, requesting a meeting between the African National Congress and the government. Even though there was no discussion about the political situation during this visit, Mandela saw it as an olive branch from the government. After this, he was given more spacious accommodation in Pollsmoor prison, Cape Town, and more opportunities for negotiation came his way. It was in early 1986 that Mandela wrote to the same minister suggesting 'talks about talks', and this marked the beginning of the process that led to his eventual unconditional release from prison, the unbanning of the ANC, free elections with the franchise given to all South Africans, black and white, and Mandela's democratic election as president in 1994. It was when Mandela, the victimized (but certainly not the victim), decided it was time to work towards reconciliation that the process advanced.

Victimhood and control

Progress towards reconciliation is jeopardized if victimhood is part of the scenery. Any desire to remain a victim needs to be resisted. Furthermore, remaining in victim mode can be a mechanism for manipulation, a guard against the feared unknown and a means (conscious or unconscious) of preventing reconciliation. There are individuals who, having suffered a trauma, remain in victim mode; for a variety of reasons (some beyond their control), they do not move on but rather sit with open wounds, sometimes eliciting guilt and generosity from those around them. In these instances, there can be an unspoken, unhealthy and uncontrollable conspiracy, which keeps the relationships static. And it is not only individuals, but groups of people or even nations who can, consciously or unconsciously, use the victim mode to provide justification for their activities.

Writing in 1991, Israeli novelist Amos Oz allows one of his characters to make the shocking link between Nazi anti-Semitism and the experience of Palestinians in Israel:

> From the bus window on the way, in the area of Mahane Yehuda market, by the light of the street lamp, he saw a black placard with the words: 'Arabs out!' He translated them into German switching Arabs with Jews, and was overwhelmed with fury.[6]

This passage makes indirect reference to the Holocaust, an event of wickedness and unparalleled barbarity leaving an horrendous blot on human history. Kenneth Cragg, formerly Assistant Bishop in Jerusalem, draws out from Oz's words the unexpected consequences of such horror:

> For many Israelis the Holocaust affords a totally inclusive alibi for whatever successful statehood requires in the effort to outlive its ravages. But not all; there are those who have identified that temptation for what it is and refuse its arguable warrant to ignore human rights in the pursuit of Jewish ones. This, for some, includes the perception that the victimized have deep in their experience a logic of retaliation, if not against the original party, then in any encounter entailed in survival. Such encounter, however external to the primary victim-experience, must carry enmity and bitterness to be released into some new equation. Palestine and Palestinian lay squarely in the path of that logic.
>
> Human history is full of such entails of pasts into presents, of wrongs undergone requiring avenging wrongs. It could hardly have been otherwise, given the sheer enormity of the Shoah.[7]

The complexity of such situations makes knee-jerk reactions dangerous, and it may appear that raising such questions when people have suffered deeply is an indication that one is not supportive of them in their pain and distress. Nothing could be further from the truth. But there is an uncontested cycle, hinted at by Oz, whereby the victims can become the victimizers.

Victims and perpetrators

The drama triangle of transactional analysis, also known as the Karpman Triangle, is recognized by therapists and counsellors as accurately describing a dynamic that can take place in human behaviour. The triangle recognizes three psychological roles that people often take in a situation. There is the victim, the persecutor and the rescuer. The victim allows himself to be punished or looked down upon; the persecutor coerces or pressurizes the victim; the rescuer intervenes out of an apparent desire to help the under-dog. As the drama plays out, people may switch roles so that the victim becomes the persecutor or the rescuer becomes the persecutor and so on. The purpose (often not recognized) of the interaction is that each member gets their psychological wishes met in a manner they believe is justified (usually drawn from something that has happened in the past), without having to recognize the harm being done in the situation as a whole. Frequently members of the triangle are acting on their own selfish needs. Such a schema may be helpful in understanding, in broad brush terms, the way people interact, and in showing how people switch roles; but it does reflect a commonly held belief that each of the three positions, victim, perpetrator and rescuer, is self-contained – in other words, that one person can be clearly identified as victim, the other clearly identified as perpetrator and the other clearly identified as rescuer. However, this is a misrepresentation and indicates a reluctance to face up to a very difficult reality. Just as it really does take two people to cause an argument, suggesting that both the 'innocent' and the 'guilty' parties need to carry their share of the blame, even though one party may be more vigorously in the wrong than the other, so too is this true in victimhood. It may well be that the perpetrator acted in a totally unjust and unacceptable way against a person who was violated through no fault of his or her own. Rwanda, the Balkans, the Holocaust, indiscriminate bombings – there are many occasions when the 'innocent' suffer. There are occasions when justice needs the perpetrator to bear the consequences of the injustice. It goes against the grain to deny innocence to those who are victimized and victims – nobody wants to add to an already heavy burden of suffering – yet the doctrine of original sin indicates that innocence has fled from the earth. The Bible itself leaves Paradise behind and moves towards the New

Jerusalem, where God offers the possibility of redemption not to the perfect but to fallen humanity.

Put starkly, the distinctions between oppressed and oppressors, victims and perpetrators, frequently used as shorthand to describe a situation, do not stand up to close scrutiny and make reconciliation impossible. As St Paul reminds his readers:

> What then? Are we any better off? No, not at all; for we have already charged that all, both Jews and Greeks, are under the power of sin, as it is written: 'There is no one who is righteous, not even one . . .'
>
> (Romans 3.9–10)

Acknowledging the sinfulness of all humanity helps prevent the cycle of the oppressed becoming the oppressor and the victim becoming the perpetrator. It also provides a challenge for those who may use victimhood as a form of manipulation. In the story of Cain and Abel (Genesis 4.1–16), in which all human beings are at one time Cain and at another Abel, God tries to break this cycle. In a masterful twist in the story, God combines his judgement against Cain the murderer with protecting Cain against the outraged supporters of the victim, by placing a protective mark on him, thereby breaking the cycle of violence:

> Cain said to the LORD, 'My punishment is greater than I can bear! Today you have driven me away from the soil, and I shall be hidden from your face; I shall be a fugitive and a wanderer on the earth, and anyone who meets me may kill me.' Then the LORD said to him, 'Not so! Whoever kills Cain will suffer a sevenfold vengeance.' And the LORD put a mark on Cain so that no one who came upon him would kill him.   (Genesis 4.13–15)

In conclusion, there can be no victims if full reconciliation is to be achieved. If there are victims in the situation, the status of their full humanity and personhood before God needs to be achieved before reconciliation can begin.

For quiet, individual reflection

1 Spend some time looking at a picture that represents Jesus as a victim, perhaps Francisco de Zurbarán's painting *Agnus Dei*, and reflect on whether Jesus was a victim or victimized. See <http://commons.wikimedia.org/wiki/Image:Francisco_de_ Zurbar%C3%A1n_006.jpg>.

2 Can you remember occasions when you have felt victimized? How did you manage the situation? What was most helpful?

3 Is Karpman's triangle helpful in describing human interaction? If it is, where would you most frequently place yourself – victim, perpetrator or rescuer?

For discussion in groups

1 Compare hymns and worship songs that describe Jesus as a victim (some examples are given below). What do they have in common and when is Jesus shown as victim or victimized?

2 Who are scapegoats in today's society, in your community, in your church, among your friends, within yourselves?

3 Discuss examples of people or peoples who, while being victimized, were not victims.

Prayer

God of mercy, God of grace, whose Son chose the path of suffering in obedience to your will, and in that choosing found liberty, freedom of spirit, and the path to resurrection: when circumstances threaten, fears assail, hope seems lost and the way seems dark, help us to tread the way that conquers misgivings; and bring us to that place of peace and contentment where faith is strengthened, fears are at rest, courage high, and where we find you with us to our journey's end.

Derek Carpenter

Examples of hymns and worship songs that refer to Jesus as 'victim'

'Alleluia, sing to Jesus'	Thou on earth both Priest and Victim
'At the Lamb's high feast'	Gives his body for the feast, Love and victim, Love the Priest
	Christ, the Lamb whose blood was shed,
	Paschal victim, Paschal bread
	Mighty Victim from on high,
	Powers of hell beneath thee lie

'Christ triumphant'	Suffering servant, scorned, ill-treated, Victim crucified
'Sing my tongue the glorious battle'	Tell how Christ the world's Redeemer, As a victim won the day
'At the Cross her station keeping'	For his people's sins, in anguish, There she saw the victim languish, Bleed in torments, bleed and die
'Alleluia, Alleluia'	He who on the Cross a victim For the world's salvation bled, Jesus Christ, the King of glory, Now is risen from the dead.

3

Forgiveness

———◆◆◆———

On the front cover of a journal on spirituality and health there was a picture of three United States ex-servicemen standing in front of the Vietnam memorial in Washington DC. One asks, 'Have you forgiven those who held you prisoner of war?' 'I will never forgive them,' replies the other. The third then comments, 'Then it seems that they still have you in prison, don't they?'

Forgiveness has been a topic of conversation high on the world's agenda over recent years, where it has been referred to in the same breath as reconciliation. The Truth and Reconciliation Commission in South Africa focused on forgiveness. Desmond Tutu's book on his work on the Commission, *No Future without Forgiveness*, suggests that forgiveness is key to reconciliation. The question, sometimes addressed, sometimes ignored, hovers around nations trying to reconstruct themselves after war and unrest – Rwanda, Sierra Leone and Northern Ireland – though it is not a word that comes naturally in the political vocabulary. Forgiveness has even been a growth area in the academic world. In the USA, there is an International Forgiveness Institute attached to the University of Wisconsin, and the John Templeton Foundation has, with others, started a multi-million dollar campaign for 'Forgiveness Research'.

Forgiveness is not just an international issue, concerned with those 'out there' – forgiveness affects each of us personally. When we are wronged, we are called upon to forgive. There are times when each of us needs to be forgiven. Perhaps the hardest task of all is when we need to forgive ourselves and when we need to accept, deep down, that we are forgiven by God. If we cannot believe that we are forgiven, we will find it hard to forgive others and to be enthusiastic about forgiveness further away. But all these forms of forgiveness are related.

Reconciliation cannot be seriously considered without taking forgiveness into account. This chapter will trace the use and understanding of forgiveness in Scripture, drawing out a distinction between forgiveness and mercy. Alongside the various understandings of forgiveness will be stories of people confronted with the tough realities of forgiveness and its role in reconciliation. Questions such as whether there are limits to forgiveness, whether there is anything that is totally unforgivable and whether there can be forgiveness without remorse will be raised. Finally, forgiveness will be considered in the world of politics and therapy, and there will be a discussion of confession as a sacrament of reconciliation (note: it is *a* sacrament of reconciliation; the Eucharist is *the* sacrament of reconciliation) and of the Church as a community of forgiveness. The chapter will conclude with a prayer written by somebody walking to their death and living forgiveness.

Forgiveness and mercy

Forgiveness and mercy are often used synonymously. But there is a difference. Many prayers invoke the mercy of God. 'Lord have mercy, Christ have mercy, Lord have mercy' is said at the beginning of the Holy Communion service. 'May God have mercy upon her soul' is frequently heard as the dead are brought before God in prayer. Mercy carries the meaning of somebody pardoning an offender, but keeping a tally of the offences. To express it in very general terms, if forgiveness is distinctive of the New Testament, mercy is distinctive of the Hebrew Scriptures, the Old Testament. Behind mercy is an understanding that there is a God of justice, who recognizes the offence that should be punished. However, instead of punishing, he has mercy. Mercy says, 'You have committed an offence and I will let you off this time, but just watch out as I will keep your offence in the back of my mind!'

However, the New Testament witnesses to the fact that God offers forgiveness because of the atonement on the cross. St Paul writes about it in this way, 'in Christ God was reconciling the world to himself, not counting their trespasses against them, and entrusting the message of reconciliation to us' (2 Corinthians 5.19). God's mercy in Christ becomes forgiveness. Forgiveness says, 'I will not allow the memory of your offence to control me or my love for you; I will lay aside your offence because I want a new relationship with you.' Forgiveness is about renewed relationships and new beginnings.

Forgiveness breaks the spiral and enables a fresh start. If reconciliation is being sought, mercy will not do – forgiveness is the only possibility.

There are examples of God's forgiveness in the Hebrew Scriptures. Through Isaiah, God is speaking words of hope to the people of Israel languishing in exile in Babylon. God is promising to restore them to their beloved land of Israel and to a fresh relationship, even though they had turned against him. Drawing upon passages already used indicating the close relationship between memory and forgiveness, the prophet Isaiah assures the people of God's forgiveness:

> Do not remember the former things, or consider the things of old. I am about to do a new thing; now it springs forth, do you not perceive it? . . . I am He who blots out your transgressions for my own sake, and I will not remember your sins.   (Isaiah 43.18–19a, 25)

Addressing the same group of people, the prophet Jeremiah says:

> No longer shall they teach one another, or say to each other, 'Know the LORD', for they shall all know me, from the least of them to the greatest, says the LORD; for I will forgive their iniquity, and remember their sin no more.   (Jeremiah 31.34)

However, forgiveness gains its widest and fullest expression in the New Testament, where Jesus shows that it has a pivotal role in reconciliation. As such, forgiveness lies at the heart of the Christian faith: it is something distinctively Christian. Christianity does not have a monopoly on it, but it has in a unique way made forgiveness a central part of its self-understanding. Jesus offers an understanding of forgiveness that was extremely radical in the climate of revenge in which he lived.

Whose forgiveness?

The Lord's prayer (Luke 11.2–4) places human forgiveness in the context of God's forgiveness. When Christians forgive, it is because God has already forgiven them: 'And forgive us our sins, for we ourselves forgive everyone indebted to us' (11.4). This important development is a reminder that the forgiveness that women and men offer to those who have given offence is a reflection of the forgiveness that

God offers to the human family. Two important consequences flow from God's forgiveness. First, as the Lord's prayer explicitly indicates, it is important to offer forgiveness to those who have given us offence in the same way that God's forgiveness is given. The story of the unmerciful servant (Matthew 18.23–35) warns readers of the consequences of not reflecting God's forgiveness in their lives. Second, human forgiveness is grounded in divine forgiveness and it can sometimes be very difficult to grasp this good news. Furthermore, an unwillingness to forgive others may well stem from an inability to accept the forgiveness that God offers. If I do not believe, at a deep level within me, that I am forgiven by God, then it is likely that I will want others to be aware of their sinfulness so that they share the same struggle as me. If I do not believe that I am forgiven, then others being in the same boat will make me feel better.

Overtly acknowledging God's role in forgiveness will enable it to happen. When, after the Second World War, a party of West German church leaders first visited Moscow to begin a dialogue with members of the Russian Orthodox Church, the German leaders expressed their sorrow over the horrors inflicted upon the Russian people by the Germans during the war. They asked to be forgiven. During the worship, there were many tears as they all remembered the cruelties and slaughter of the time. Then the Russians said 'God may forgive you' and they kissed the crosses of the German church leaders and asked for their blessings.

The Russian Christians were not saying 'God may forgive you, but we cannot'; rather they were saying that God would give them the strength to forgive and overcome their traumatic memories.[1] By kissing the crosses and asking for their blessings, they were accepting the German leaders as their leaders. Forgiveness thus forges a way forward and breaks the spiral of vengeance and retribution.

Is there a limit to forgiveness?

When Peter asks Jesus how many times he should forgive somebody who sins against him, he receives a reply that would have sounded as outrageously generous then as it does now:

> 'As many as seven times?' Jesus said to him, 'Not seven times, but, I tell you, seventy-seven times.'   (Matthew 18.21–22)

In other words, there is no limit to the times one forgives.

Place Jesus' claim that there is no limit to forgiveness alongside another text. When Jesus was in dispute with the scribes from Jerusalem, he was accused of doing his works under the influence of Beelzebub. Jesus responded:

> 'Truly I tell you, people will be forgiven for their sins and whatever blasphemies they utter; but whoever blasphemes against the Holy Spirit can never have forgiveness, but is guilty of an eternal sin' – for they had said, 'He has an unclean spirit.' (Mark 3.28–30)

The unpardonable sin here is the rejection of the Spirit's work in God's Kingdom and therefore the rejection of God. Those who obstinately reject Jesus, despite witnessing his works and the context in which they are taking place, are placing themselves beyond the salvation of God until they turn back towards God. The people of God, who knowingly reject what God is doing because they fear what will happen to them if they recognize God's hand at work, are warned in the Gospels about judgement. Their offence is greater than those who reject God because they do not know or understand what they are doing.

Two aspects of the limits to forgiveness are raised here. One is the reasonably straightforward question about frequency of forgiveness. The other is whether some sins are so serious that they can never be forgiven. Whether there are limits to forgiveness, in particular in the latter sense, has always been a question of dispute. It is seen at its most harrowing in the Holocaust. Simon Wiesenthal, well known for his organization, which hunted Nazi war criminals after the Second World War, was himself imprisoned in a concentration camp. While a prisoner, he was taken to the bedside of a dying SS soldier who, overwhelmed by guilt, graphically described his crimes and asked Wiesenthal, as a Jew, for forgiveness. After hearing the soldier and being deeply troubled by what he heard, Wiesenthal simply left in silence. Nobody could criticize Wiesenthal for his action, though Wiesenthal himself subsequently questioned whether he had acted correctly. Wiesenthal was confronted with the most difficult of situations – he had suffered horrendous treatment at the hands of the Nazis and yet the soldier's request evoked from deep within him the tortured question of forgiveness.

Questions about forgiveness arise with any crimes against humanity. On a less grand scale, though with no less serious consequences for those who suffer as a result, are senseless crimes against individuals: when a gang of young people senselessly beat to death a father enjoying a game of cricket with his son in the park; when a young father is stabbed to death because he objected to people damaging his car.

However, some difficult and emotive questions arise, especially with the Holocaust, which highlights sharp questions about forgiveness. If God does side with those who are oppressed and victimized, then would it not be a betrayal to forgive those who commit such monstrous crimes against humanity? Is it right to move on as though these crimes are forgotten? Professor Ulrich Simon, drawing on the gospel's acknowledgement that some sins cannot be forgiven, is clear:

> There is a sin against Man and Spirit which Christ declared to be unforgivable, and Auschwitz is this sin against Man and Spirit. It is the supreme act of blasphemy, and the men and tools who caused it neither desire nor can receive the forgiveness of their sin.[2]

In many ways it is disrespectful for those who have not had to undergo such horrors even to raise the question of forgiveness, and yet if we are to listen seriously to the spirit of the gospel, then the answer, hard as it may be in so many instances, has to be that God's forgiveness is beyond human understanding. Isaiah hints at God's priority when he reminds the Israelites, exiled because of their disobedience and faithlessness:

> Can a woman forget her nursing child, or show no compassion for the child of her womb? Even these may forget, yet I will not forget you. See, I have inscribed you on the palm of my hands; your walls are continually before me.   (Isaiah 49.15–16)

Even when Israel had forgotten God, God would not forget Israel. Even when Israel had turned her back on the Lord, the Lord did not turn his back on Israel, just as a mother cannot forget the child she has carried and borne. There comes a point at which those who have been the object of wrongdoing and crimes need to forgive, otherwise, like the former US serviceman in front of the Vietnam memorial, they continue to remain imprisoned by those who have wronged them. This is hard to hear for those who have suffered and have been victimized, but how else can one walk the path of reconciliation? Volf describes this dilemma in these words:

> My thought was pulled in two different directions by the blood of the innocent crying out to God and by the blood of God's lamb offered for the guilty. How does one remain loyal both to the demand of the oppressed and to the gift of forgiveness that the Crucified offered to the perpetrators?[3]

In other words, God holds in his love both the person who is wronged and the one who inflicts the wrong. Some of these uncomfortable questions will recur as we consider a story that lies at the heart of St Luke's Gospel and has an enormous amount to teach about forgiveness and reconciliation.

Forgiveness breaks down barriers

The story of the 'All-loving Father' in St Luke (remember it is known misleadingly as the 'Prodigal Son' – misleading because it places the emphasis on the wrongdoing of the son rather than the abundant love of the father) tells the story of a son who took his share of his father's property, squandered all that he had in dissolute living, and then found himself in great need (Luke 15.11–32). He then comes to his senses and decides to return to his father, full of remorse, and offer himself as a hired hand. His father sees him coming at a distance, rushes towards and embraces his returning son. The son is forgiven and embraced by his father even before his father hears his words of repentance. Some of those hearing the story for the first time would have been outraged by the behaviour of the younger son and the way in which he was welcomed back; others would have been moved to repentance.

The story of the All-loving Father is so important in the understanding of forgiveness and reconciliation that some time needs to be spent on it. For Luke, forgiveness of sins is central to his theology and synonymous with salvation; accordingly, the story lies at the heart of St Luke's understanding of Jesus Christ's actions and identity. So too the 'embrace' in Miroslav Volf's insightful book, *Exclusion and Embrace*, is that of the father towards his son. Some of the reflections on this passage are drawn from Volf's book.

The father's initial response to his returning son was to embrace and receive him unconditionally, even before the son had had a chance to express his remorse. However, the son did then make his confession, 'Father, I have sinned against heaven and before you; I am no longer worthy to be called your son' (Luke 15.21), after which (or maybe even during which) the father promptly reinstated him as his son:

> But the father said to the slaves, 'Quickly, bring out a robe – the best one – and put it on him; put a ring on his finger and sandals on his feet. And get the fatted calf and kill it, and let us eat and celebrate; for this son of mine was dead and is alive again; he was lost and is found!' And they began to celebrate. (Luke 15.22–24)

The son needed to make a confession to complete the reconciliation between him and his father, but it was necessary more for the son's sake than the father's, who had already embraced his son. The father's actions and the younger son's waywardness are criticized by the elder brother, who believes that he is being unfairly treated – and many readers' sympathies go out to the elder brother. But what the elder brother fails to understand is that the father's relationship to his sons is not shaped by what they do, but by who they are. For all that the younger brother had done, reprehensible as it may have been, he was still his father's son. The younger son, though restored, was not reinstated into all his former privileges; he is not exactly the same son as he was before his departure, but now he is the 'son-that-was-dead-and-is-alive-again'.[4] For the father, the fact that he was his son was more significant in his relationship with him than what he had done. Of course, the moral activity of the younger son is not irrelevant, but it is not as important as the father's relationship with his son. Luke's Gospel is full of Jesus' encounters, especially with those rejected by the 'establishment'. These exemplify the important fact that relationship is prior to all else. It is the father's forgiveness, fuelled by his love, that creates a climate for this to happen. In addition, the father's forgiveness breaks through the narrow way in which contemporary culture would have viewed the incident and provides a new way. Volf sums this up:

> Flexible order? Changing identities? The world of fixed rules and stable identities is the world of the older brother. The father destabilizes this world – and draws his older son's anger upon himself. The father's

most basic commitment is not to rules and given identities but to his sons whose lives are too complex to be regulated by fixed rules and whose identities are too dynamic to be defined once for all. Yet he does not give up the rules and the order once for all. Guided by the indestructible love which makes space in the self for others in their alterity, which invites the others who have transgressed to return, which creates hospitable conditions for their confession, and rejoices over their presence, the father keeps re-configuring the order without destroying it so as to maintain it as an order of embrace rather than exclusion.[5]

One man whose attitude of forgiveness changed the order of conflict was Gordon Wilson. A man of deep Christian faith, in 1987 he was attending the Remembrance Day commemoration in Enniskillen, Northern Ireland, with his daughter Marie, when a Provisional IRA bomb exploded, burying Gordon and Marie beneath the rubble. Marie died, along with ten others, but Gordon was pulled out from the rubble and survived. On that same evening, he described with great anguish on the BBC his last conversation with his daughter as they lay beneath the rubble:

She held my hand tightly and gripped me as hard as she could. She said, 'Daddy, I love you very much.' Those were her last words to me, and those were the last words I ever heard her say. But I bear no ill will. I bear no grudge. Dirty sort of talk is not going to bring her back to life. She was a great wee lassie. She loved her profession. She was a pet. She's dead. She's in heaven and we shall meet again. I will pray for these men tonight and every night.[6]

Gordon Wilson's forgiveness of his daughter's murderers undoubtedly prevented revenge attacks by Loyalist paramilitaries. On many occasions he met with Sinn Fein and even the Provisional IRA. His heartfelt words of forgiveness had an enormous impact and would have added a lot in the movement for reconciliation.

Is remorse necessary for forgiveness?

At the crucifixion, even as the nails were being driven in, Jesus said, 'Father, forgive them, for they do not know what they are doing' (Luke 23.34). In these words, Jesus exemplifies, in his death, his understanding of forgiveness. The way in which people die can summarize the way in which they live. Forgiving those who have wronged one is an act of freedom, a denial of victimhood: forgiving those who are killing one is the ultimate sign of freedom and liberation. If it is not possible to forgive until the perpetrator of evil confesses and shows remorse, then the person being wronged will still be under the control of the perpetrator and locked into victimhood. Jesus was never freer than when he was on the cross. Jesus' action is the ultimate example of forgiveness, when reconciliation was brought about between humanity and God. What is significant here is that the guilt and condemnation of those responsible is not a precondition for forgiveness. If they had known what they were doing, it would have been different, but Jesus did not ask for the repentance of those nailing him to the cross before uttering those words of forgiveness. Yet the way in which he showed forgiveness and compassion and embodied reconciliation elicited a response of wonder, amazement and faith:

> When the centurion saw what had taken place, he praised God and said, 'Certainly this man was innocent.' (Luke 23.47)

A remarkable example of a person praying for forgiveness, even though there was no remorse, is to be found in the Civil Rights Movement in the USA. In the 1960s, schools that had been for white children only were desegregated. One black child, six-year-old Ruby Bridges, attended her school alone, escorted by police past angry white mobs. Ruby sat in a classroom all day with one teacher. American child-psychiatrist Robert Coles came to know Ruby and questioned her about a report from her teacher that the little girl's lips were moving as she walked passed the baying white mobs. When Coles asked Ruby what she was saying, she replied:

> 'I was saying a prayer for them.'
> 'Ruby, you pray for the people there?'
> 'Oh yes.'
> 'Why do you do that?'
> 'Because they need praying for.'
> 'Why you especially?'
> 'Because if you're going through what they're doing to you, you're the one who should be praying for them.'
>   And then she quoted to me what she had heard in church. The minister said that Jesus went through a lot of trouble, and he said

about the people who were causing the trouble, 'Forgive them because they don't know what they're doing.' And now little Ruby was saying this in the 1960s, about the people in the streets of New Orleans. How is someone like me supposed to understand that, psychologically or any other way?[7]

Just as the sight of what the centurion saw and heard elicited a response of wonder, amazement and faith, so too seeing and hearing about Ruby elicited from Dr Coles a response of wonder and amazement – faith too?

Another person who, using Jesus' words of forgiveness on the cross, was able to transform the situation in which he found himself was Bishop Leonard Wilson of Singapore. Bishop Wilson was imprisoned during the time of the Japanese occupation and on 13 October, 1946, he broadcast his story on the BBC:

I was interned in March, 1943, and sent to Changi jail . . . It is not my purpose to relate the tortures inflicted upon us, but rather to tell you of some of the spiritual experiences of that ordeal. I knew that this was to be a challenge to my courage, my faith and my love . . . I did not like to use the words 'Father forgive them.' It seemed too blasphem-ous to use our Lord's words, but I felt them, and I said, 'Father, I know these men are doing their duty. Help them to see that I am innocent.' When I muttered, 'Forgive them', I wondered how far I was being dramatic, and if I really meant it, because I looked at their faces as they stood around and took it in turn to flog, and their faces were hard and cruel and some of them were evidently enjoying their cruelty. But, by the grace of God I saw those men not as they were, but as they had been. Once they were little children playing with their brothers and sisters and happy in their parents' love, in those far-off days before they had been conditioned by their false nationalist ideals, and it is hard to hate little children . . . And so I saw them, not as they were, but as they were capable of becoming, redeemed by the power of Christ, and I knew that it was only common sense to say 'Forgive.'[8]

One of the similarities shared by the stories of Ruby Bridges, Leonard Wilson and the Russian Christians who met the German church lead-ers is that the depth of their faith in God enabled them to offer forgiveness. Forgiveness becomes a political possibility for black Christians in the USA and the Russian Christians because of the depth of their faith in God. As will become apparent, forgiveness is not prominent in politics, which means that politics alone will not enable a breakthrough when searching for reconciliation. Countries in which Truth and Reconciliation Commissions have had a reasonable success in bringing about reconciliation, namely South Africa and Sierra Leone, have not only had religious leaders in high profile positions on the Commissions, but are also in countries where the Christian faith is widely practised and where the vocabulary of forgiveness will be known.

So is remorse necessary for forgiveness? If this were the case, then those unable or unwilling to be remorseful would still hold those whom they have wronged in their power. Forgiveness is an act of liberation for all concerned. In the story of the All-loving Father, remorse and regret were essential for the younger son because he had realized that he had done wrong. It was necessary in order that the son could experience forgiveness, but the father's forgiveness was not conditional upon the son's remorse. But in the cases of Jesus on the cross and Ruby Bridges facing the howling mobs, remorse was not necessary.

The same view is expressed in the final report of the Sierra Leone Truth and Reconciliation Commission, published in August 2007. In a similar spirit to the South African TRC, the Sierra Leone Commission was convened to help the country move forward after 11 years of bitter fighting. The Commission's chairman, United Methodist Church Bishop Joseph Humper (note that a Christian leader was again, like Archbishop Tutu, asked to lead the task), wrote in his preface:

> Reconciliation is strengthened through acknowledgment and forgiveness, those who have confronted the past will have no problem in acknowledging their roles in the conflict and expressing remorse for such roles. Where the act of forgiveness is genuine it does not matter whether the perpetrator declines to express remorse.[9]

It is in the environment created by forgiveness that justice and making amends can be pursued. It may be easier for the person who has been wronged to hear words of remorse and repentance before offering forgiveness, but it is not necessary. Forgiveness can break the cycle of hatred, bitterness and resentment and open up new possibilities. Sadly, it hardly figures in politics, as we shall now consider.

Forgiveness and politics

The social theorist Hannah Arendt wrote:

> The discoverer of the role of forgiveness in the realm of human affairs was Jesus of Nazareth. The fact that he made this discovery in a religious context and articulated it in religious language is no reason to take it any less seriously in a strictly secular sense. It has been in the nature of our tradition of political thought (and for reasons we cannot explore here) to be highly selective and to exclude from articulate conceptualization a great variety of authentic political experiences, among which we need not be surprised to find some of an even elementary nature. Certain aspects of the teaching of Jesus of Nazareth which are not primarily related to the Christian message but sprang from experiences in the small and closely knit community of his followers, bent on challenging the public authorities in Israel, certainly belong among them, even though they have been neglected because of their allegedly exclusively religious nature.[10]

It has already been pointed out that forgiveness in politics has usually been introduced through the medium of faith and through the mediation of religious figures such as Archbishop Desmond Tutu when chairing the Truth and Reconciliation Commission in South Africa and Bishop Joseph Humper in Sierra Leone. These organs of forgiveness and reconciliation used in pursuit of a political end, namely to help a broken and divided nation to be drawn together and move forward with a shared vision, are rare indeed. Generally, political engagement is characterized by a cycle of criticism and retaliation. Recent, genuine attempts by some politicians, usually freshly in post, to rise above the adversarial climate of political engagement have come to nothing. Forgiveness is regarded as a sign of weakness rather than strength, and to give a political enemy a political advantage would be tantamount to selling one's political birthright. Furthermore, if the language of forgiveness and reconciliation is sought in politics, it is important that it should not be an empty gesture but rather rooted in the truth in order to bring about change. The problem that arises when it is not rooted in truth became apparent during an incident in the South African TRC process.

A former security policeman, Gideon Niewoudt, was seeking amnesty for the murder in the mid 1980s of an activist called Siphiwe

Mtimkulu. Prior to the amnesty hearing, the police had done every-thing possible to protect themselves, which included lying: even in telling the truth, there are ways of keeping the real truth obscured. In a television documentary on this issue, Niewoudt is filmed visiting the Mtimkulu family to ask for forgiveness. Siphiwe's mother, because of her faith in God, is reluctantly willing to grant forgiveness, but other members of the family were not so sure, and persisted in ques-tioning Niewoudt about responsibility for Siphiwe's poisoning and shooting.

After a while, Siphiwe's young son, who had been in the shadows of the room, snatched a heavy object and threw it at Niewoudt, injur-ing his head. Niewoudt was rushed to hospital. The younger son later said, 'I could not listen to him continuing to tell lies.'[11]

In political discourse in particular, even the truth can be used as a means of deception. Forgiveness is the language of faith, and in a number of disputes, while the politicians negotiate in the glare of publicity, men and women of faith speak a different language in the background, opening up possibilities of reconciliation. This was certainly the case in Northern Ireland and continues to be the case in Israel/Palestine.

A sacrament of reconciliation

In the story of the All-loving Father, the younger son recognized that he had done wrong and wanted to admit his remorse for his actions. He realized that his father had forgiven him, but in order to experi-ence forgiveness, in order to feel forgiven, it was necessary for him to express sorrow for his actions. He was willing to pay a penalty or, using the language of the Church, to undertake a penance. The son said, 'I will get up and go to my father, and I will say to him, "Father, I have sinned against heaven and before you; I am no longer worthy to be called your son; treat me like one of your hired hands"' (Luke 15.18–19).

For reconciliation to happen, there needs to be ritual. It has already been pointed out that the Eucharist is the sacrament for those who are reconciled, and on the way to being reconciled, but the confession of sins, a sacrament of reconciliation, is a ritual that provides the environment for the path that the younger son in Luke 15 needed to take in order to experience the forgiveness generously offered by the father. It is not my purpose to encourage everybody to the confessional, though many would find this a liberating experience, but to point out the need for an environment where people can grapple with sin, offer repentance and experience forgiveness in order to be part of the process of reconciliation.

The sacrament of reconciliation (which will be explored more fully later) is the Eucharist. Being able to lay one's sin before God on a regular basis and hearing the words of absolution given at the Eucharist brings a powerful awareness of our own inadequacies and sinfulness set alongside God's love and assurance of forgiveness. It places our fallenness in the context of love, hope and transformation.

One of the presenting issues sparking the rebellion within the Church in the sixteenth century that is known as the Reformation was the practice and understanding of penance and forgiveness. How can a person be in a right relationship with God? The Church had been using the practice of penance to gain acceptability before God, giving its priests the task of being mediators of God's forgiveness. However, the system was being abused and it was Martin Luther, himself wracked with guilt and, at the same time, desperately searching for the God of grace, who became the public face of rebellion. Luther fought against the teaching that undertaking acts of penance was the basis for God's forgiveness and, consequently, for absolution. God's forgiveness is freely given to those who genuinely seek it, and believing in God's promise was the only requirement for the appropriation of God's grace. An outcome of this rebellion was that in those churches that turned their backs on Rome, auricular confession was no longer practised, being replaced by a general confession of sins in worship or personal confession in private prayers. The disadvantage of this practice is that, while recognizing that God's forgiveness is freely given, it is not enough. It is important and therapeutic that we can say what is in our hearts to another person and hear from him or her the reality of God's forgiveness. That person is not offering forgiveness, but is a channel through which God can work in confirming the reality of God's grace. Men and women need to articulate their guilt and be assured that they are forgiven. Returning to the younger son of the All-loving Father, even though his father had forgiven him, the son needed to say his words of confession to seal, for himself, God's forgiveness, and he needed to know that he was forgiven.

Carl Jung asserts that the absence of the confessional in Protestant churches has adversely affected spiritual well-being. There is a dearth of places where people can talk about the deep issues, which are matters of the soul as much as the heart. In many ways the counsellor and therapist have provided the listening ear previously associated with the Church. They have the skills to touch the fragmented self and enable reintegration. But although the therapist may be able to help a person with their guilt and shame, can she or he help a person with their sin?

There has been a tendency in the West to think that talking in order to understand a problematic situation can solve it. Philosopher Isaiah Berlin traces the roots of this belief back to Plato, where the conviction 'that reality is wholly knowable, and that knowledge and only knowledge liberates, and absolute knowledge liberates absolutely' can be found.[12] In other words, the more we can understand a situation and why we (or somebody else) reacted in a particular way, the better we can feel and the more successfully we can manage its difficulty. This may be true for many situations, but certainly not for all. Forgiveness is not the same as understanding – we cannot 'think', 'feel' or 'understand' sin away. The story of Jesus Christ makes it clear that God does not offer forgiveness because of his knowledge but because of his love. God's forgiveness breaks into the world, it does not simply well up from within, and in order that it is appropriated, there needs to be something that touches the heart and soul as well as the mind and emotions.

The sign that the sacrament of reconciliation is completed in a person or, to put it differently, the sign that God's forgiveness has been appropriated, is renewal. Perhaps the finest example of this can be seen in the meeting between Jesus and Peter after the resurrection. In the first recorded conversation between the two since Peter denied that he knew Jesus (John 18.25–27), Jesus said to Peter, ' "Simon, son of John, do you love me more than these?" He said to him, "Yes, Lord; you know that I love you." Jesus said to him, "Feed my lambs" ' (John 21.15). Three times Jesus asked Peter whether he loved him, three times Peter insisted that he did and on each occasion Jesus gave him an extra responsibility – 'Feed my lambs . . . Tend my sheep . . . Feed my sheep'. Jesus was restoring Peter. By asking him the question three times, Jesus was reminding Peter of the three times that he had denied him. He was raising his guilty past, not in order to condemn or control Peter, but in order to open up new possibilities and offer him a new future. The purpose of the sacrament of reconciliation is not to hold people to account in guilt, but to open them up to a new future, recognizing that the very energy that leads them to sin can be used by God to lead them to great things. This is something that is distinctive of God's forgiveness through Jesus Christ, namely that the ultimate aim of the encounter is not condemnation but renewal. St Paul develops this in his second letter to the Corinthians when he writes, 'My grace is sufficient for you, for power is made perfect in weakness' (2 Corinthians 12.9). When a violin that has been broken is repaired, it can, if properly restored, make a purer sound than before it was broken. God's forgiveness is able to restore human beings in a similar way – as he did with Peter. This is the purpose of sacraments of reconciliation.

The Church as a community of forgiveness

The Church is a community that is both forgiven and in the process of being forgiven, and it is called to reflect this reality to the world. In a society that permits everything but forgives nothing, the Church has a particularly daunting task to combat the fear that comes from not recognizing one's forgiveness. The Church needs to provide the environment where its members can share their joys and triumphs as well as their weaknesses and vulnerabilities, and the sharing needs to be done in such a way as to encourage others to want to be part of the community. As such, the Church is a sacrament of reconciliation. Whenever the Church fails to show itself as a forgiven community, then it is no longer fulfilling its vocation. There is nothing wrong in the Church being a community of struggle, but if there is a spirit that leads to exclusion rather than inclusion, then it needs to turn to deeper prayer to ask whether it really is following the Spirit of God or whether it has succumbed to the spirit of the world. The Church is the place where the inbreaking of forgiveness is celebrated and recognized as an act of God and a sign of the Kingdom.

The Church is also a forgiving community that constantly points to God's forgiveness, naming it as a gift from God regardless of where it is witnessed. The Church has a role in making available the sacraments, which help make God's forgiveness real to people. The Church's role in Truth and Reconciliation Commissions in South Africa and Sierra Leone, as well as in Northern Ireland and the Middle East, is a reminder that forgiveness, which is more a virtue of faith than an activity in politics, can nevertheless play an important role in politics. Thus, the Church also needs to be a place of welcome and encouragement to those outside who are wanting God's forgiveness but are unable to find it. The Church, then, needs to be a place that models both forgiving and being forgiven; and as we shall discover in the last chapter, this can be a difficult task.

Forgiveness is the breaking in of a new order of relating. It involves seeing the world reconstructed and lived from the perspective of the reality that is profoundly simple to hear but often extremely difficult to live, namely that God forgives each of us. Our taking hold of this truth is reflected in the way each person is able to forgive others. The Greek word used for forgiveness in the New Testament means to 'let go'. Forgiveness means letting go of the wrong and being willing to move forward. This letting go is making sure that one is not controlled or imprisoned by the wrong, as the US ex-serviceman was at the beginning of this chapter. We end this chapter with a remarkable prayer that comes from the concentration camp at Ravensbrück, where 92,000 women and children died. This prayer, which is both glorious and challenging, offered by a nameless woman and placed beside the dead body of a child, responds in a way that little else can to the question raised earlier about whether some wrongs are beyond forgiveness. It also helps us understand the miracle that we celebrate over Good Friday and Easter and it reaches the heart of forgiveness:

> O Lord, remember not only the men and women of good will, but also those of ill will. But do not remember all the suffering they have inflicted on us; remember the fruits we have borne, thanks to this suffering – our comradeship, our loyalty, our humility, our courage, our generosity, the greatness of heart which has grown out of all this; and when they come to the judgement, let all the fruits that we have borne be their forgiveness.[13]

For quiet, individual reflection

1 With which of the characters in the story of the All-loving Father (Luke 15.11–32) do you identify most closely?

2 Look at Rembrandt's painting *The Return of the Prodigal Son.* What particular aspects of forgiveness strike you? (See <www. wga.hu/frames-e.html?/html/r/rembran/painting/biblic3/ prodig2.html>)

3 Reflect on times when you have forgiven and been forgiven, and the way in which your relationship with the person(s) was changed.

For discussion in groups

1 Do you think that there are some crimes that are beyond the forgiveness of God?

2 Do you agree with George Herbert when he writes, 'He who cannot forgive breaks the bridge over which he himself must pass'?

3 In what ways is your church a community of forgiveness?

4 Take some time to discuss and then pray the prayer from Ravensbrück.

Prayer

O Lord, remember not only the men and women of good will, but also those of ill will. But do not remember all the suffering they have inflicted on us; remember the fruits we have borne, thanks to this suffering – our comradeship, our loyalty, our humility, our courage, our generosity, the greatness of heart which has grown out of all this; and when they come to the judgement, let all the fruits that we have borne be their forgiveness.

Prayer written by an unknown prisoner in
Ravensbrück concentration camp

4

Reaching out to the other

Reconciliation is not possible unless there is an embracing of the 'other' – the other person, the other idea, the otherness of ourselves, the otherness of God. The other is the one outside of ourselves. That human beings can stretch beyond themselves in this way differentiates them from animals. The depth to which otherness is embedded in reconciliation is demonstrated by the fact that the Greek word for reconciliation used in the New Testament (*katallasso*) has at its heart the Greek word for 'other' (*allos*). Thus, reconciliation is centred on a relationship with the other.

Yet today, the cult of the individual militates against otherness. Contemporary British society encourages us to be so focused on ourselves and our own needs that there is little or no awareness of the other, and when there is, the other can be regarded as an enemy and a threat. Lack of awareness of the other can be seen in a whole range of scenarios, from the personal to the spatial to the political. The mantra that people should live life in such a way that their needs are always being met sounds the death-knell to community and creativity and undermines what lies at the heart of the gospel. It is becoming more common in crowded places, such as shops and streets, to find people so centred on what they want to do that they end up blocking the passage of others, as though unaware, or not caring, that others want to pass. In a society that prides itself on being tolerant and open, there is a real reluctance to take seriously those whose beliefs and politics stem from other ideological roots. The stranger and the alien are regarded with suspicion. This, as we shall see, is in stark contrast to ancient Israel, whose laws ensured that embracing the other lay at the heart of their society. (The ancient Israelites were not perfect at following this principle – it fell to the prophets to remind them of their obligations.)

However, otherness is not acceptable on its own. A willingness to embrace otherness needs to be set in the context of another deeply human and God-given impulse, which is a desire for communion with other people and with God. Human beings are made for communion – we need each other if we are to flourish as human beings. John Donne, in his well-known passage, points to this when he writes, 'No man is an island entire of itself.' The significance of relationships for many Africans is expressed in the saying, 'I am because we are'; a Zulu saying expresses it in a different way, 'A person becomes a person because of people.'

Human beings are also made for communion with God. St Augustine reflects on the relationship with God when he cries out 'our hearts are restless until they find their rest in thee'. The Psalmist reminds us, 'As a deer longs for flowing streams, so my soul longs for you, O God' (Psalm 42). The need for relationship with others and the desire for communion with God are bound up with each other.

The dynamic between otherness and communion is seen perfectly constituted in the Trinity, in the relationship between God as Father, Son and Holy Spirit. Here the otherness of each of the persons is respected, and it leads to a perfect communion of love. Otherness needs to lead to communion and unity.

After locating the issue of otherness in the Scriptures, this chapter will explore the central theme of otherness and will illustrate various responses to it. It will consider embracing the other, excluding the other and dehumanizing the other. It will then look in more detail at the dynamic between otherness and communion.

Otherness and the Scriptures – God's unique relationship

Hospitality has always been a mark of Middle Eastern society, and welcoming the other is strong in the Bible. Genesis 18.1–8 recounts the story of Abraham entertaining three strangers. Abraham welcomes, feeds and entertains them and later discovers that they bring news from God. In a commentary on this event, the author of the letter to the Hebrews writes, 'Do not neglect to show hospitality to strangers, for by doing that some have entertained angels without knowing it' (Hebrews 13.2). But the Israelites were commanded to go even further. Through its treatment of the 'other', Israel was commanded by God to create a radical society, which was to take particular notice of those considered to be on the edge. The Israelites were to remember that they had experienced being of the edge, that they too were aliens, and they were to recite a particular formula recalling their experience of alienation when they made an offering to God at their harvest:

> When the priest takes the basket from your hand and sets it down before the altar of the LORD your God, you shall make this response before the LORD your God: 'A wandering Aramean was my ancestor; he went down to Egypt and lived there as an alien, few in number, and there he became a great nation, mighty and populous.'
> (Deuteronomy 26.4–5)

It went further still. Not only were the Israelites to take special notice and care of the other, but their identity as God's people depended upon it. In this way, the land, which belonged to God, would produce a people who were a great blessing to their neighbours. One test of the goodness of the people of Israel, of the quality of their relationship to God and of the depth of their worship, was the way in which they treated foreigner, alien, orphan and widow. Whenever they fell short, they were lambasted by the prophets. Amos famously tells the people that their worship, elaborate and heartfelt as it appeared to be, meant nothing to God because of their neglect of the other, because of the way they were allowing the poor to be exploited:

> I hate, I despise your festivals, and I take no delight in your solemn assemblies. Even though you offer me your burnt-offerings and grain-offerings, I will not accept them; and the offerings of well-being of your fatted animals I will not look upon. Take away from me the noise of your songs; I will not listen to the melody of your harps. But let justice roll down like waters, and righteousness like an ever-flowing stream.
> (Amos 5.21–24)

Three centuries later Malachi issues similar warnings, showing how deeply care for the other is engrained in the faith of the Hebrews:

> Then I will draw near to you for judgement; I will be swift to bear witness against the sorcerers, against the adulterers, against those who swear falsely, against those who oppress the hired workers in their wages, the widow, and the orphan, against those who thrust aside the alien, and do not fear me, says the LORD of hosts.
> (Malachi 3.5)

The attitude towards the other is all the more significant because it points to something important about God that is unique to the Judeo–Christian tradition, namely that God is both wholly 'other' while at the same time intimately involved in his creation.

Transcendence is the word often used to describe God's 'otherness', and people respond to God's transcendence in worship by referring to his awe and holiness. God's otherness and transcendence are apparent when Moses approached God with the people of Israel in the wilderness: they had to undergo rituals of cleansing before they could encounter the Lord. Anybody who so much as touched the holy mountain would face death.

> On the morning of the third day there was thunder and lightning, as well as a thick cloud on the mountain, and a blast of a trumpet so loud that all the people who were in the camp trembled. Moses brought the people out of the camp to meet God. They took their stand at the foot of the mountain. Now Mount Sinai was wrapped in smoke, because the LORD had descended upon it in fire; the smoke went up like the smoke of a kiln, while the whole mountain shook violently.
>
> (Exodus 19.16–18)

Similarly, Isaiah 6.1–4 offers a vision of the awesome and holy nature of God when the prophet Isaiah feels completely overwhelmed by the Lord, seated on his throne, 'high and lofty'. God's otherness is expressed in God's total separation from his creation. God is Creator and is not dependent upon his creation.

At the same time as being totally other, God is intimately involved. In the creation story, God, the Creator, wanders through the garden in the cool of the day to speak with Adam (Genesis 3.8). God leads his people out of slavery towards the Promised Land when he sees how much they are suffering, and he protects them from the Egyptians (Exodus 14). A recurrent theme in the Hebrew Scriptures is God's anger towards his people when they break the agreement (Covenant) they have made with God, and God's welcoming them back when they return to him. The marvellous poetry in Isaiah 40—54 is a testimony to God's delight that Israel is returning; and God will go to any lengths to enable their return:

> I am about to do a new thing; now it springs forth, do you not perceive it? I will make a way in the wilderness and rivers in the desert. The wild animals will honour me, the jackals and the ostriches; for I

give water in the wilderness, rivers in the desert, to give drink to my chosen people, the people whom I formed for myself so that they might declare my praise.   (Isaiah 43.19–21)

God's being wholly other and yet intimately involved is most particularly embodied in the person of Jesus Christ, through the mystery of his being fully human and fully God. Fra Angelico's painting, *The Adoration of the Magi*, exquisitely depicts this mystery as the powerful and influential magi pay homage to a 'mere' baby.[1] What is it that they are honouring – a gift who is both intimately involved and yet wholly other? By his nature, Jesus shows God's ultimate involvement in and love for the world through his willingness to die for it; and at the same time, the resurrection shows God's total independence and otherness to his creation. No other religion has this unique dynamic at its centre – indeed, many religions regard it as a scandal. The otherness of God combined with his intimate involvement with creation seen in its ultimate expression in the life, death and resurrection of Jesus Christ is important for the theme of reconciliation because Jesus, God's gift to the world, is the embodiment of reconciliation.

Embracing the other

Cahal Daly was Roman Catholic Archbishop of Armagh during the height of the troubles in Northern Ireland. He spent much of his time dealing in a very direct way with issues of reconciliation. In one conversation, he demonstrated the significance of a willingness to embrace the other as part of the process. He spoke of two people (A and B) trying to reach a point of reconciliation. It was important, he said, for A and B to walk in parallel tracks, A telling B about the issues, dilemmas, struggles and difficulties A was facing. Next, the two needed to walk back along the same track, B telling A about the issues B was facing. Finally, the two needed to walk along the same track telling each other what fears they had about agreeing.

Archbishop Daly's simple story contains an enormous amount of wisdom and insight. First, it is important to be able to talk to and communicate with the person with whom we are in dispute; there is a need to have a climate in which open and honest conversation is possible. Second, there needs to be a willingness for each party to listen to the other, which means respecting the person as a human being even though we may not agree with his or her views. Real listening is a dangerous and potentially subversive activity, as psychotherapist Carl Rogers points out:

> If you really understand another person in this way, if you are willing to enter his private world and see the way life appears to him, without any attempt to make evaluative judgements, you run the risk of being changed yourself. You might see it his way, you might find yourself influenced in your attitudes or your personality. This risk of being changed is one of the most frightening prospects most of us can face. If I enter, as fully as I am able, into the private world of a neurotic or psychotic individual, isn't there a risk that I might become lost in that world? . . . The great majority of us could not *listen*; we would find ourselves compelled to *evaluate*, because listening would seem too dangerous. So the first requirement is courage, and we do not always have it.[2]

The church is ideally situated to be a place where both listening and conversation can happen. There are many wonderful and saintly people within churches who are gifted listeners, able to support men and women in the dilemmas and pains through which they are passing. But is the church a place of *listening and conversation*?

The church where I served as parish priest, in a multi-cultural and multi-lingual area of northern Zambia, was made up of people whose mother tongues were ci-Bemba and ci-Chewa (from Zambia), Tamil and Malayalam (from India and Sri Lanka) and English. English was the only common language, but it was the language of the minority. The different languages could be heard in services, so that all language groupings would be able to worship in their mother tongue, even if it was only for a few minutes. So parts of the Eucharist would be sung in ci-Bemba, the congregation would listen to a song in Tamil, prayers might be said in Malayalam and readings in English. Even if worshippers did not understand the language in which a song was sung, they would listen to somebody worship God in their own language, realizing they were worshipping on behalf of all. Listening to others worshipping God in their language on behalf of all had a profound effect on all present, as their listening showed a deep respect of the culture of the other. If this happen within church, it could also happen outside. Listening often turned into conversation at some point, as worshippers would speak about their singing or their listening. One elderly English lady who did not understand the local languages commented that she did not understand the language in which the 'Lamb of God' was sung, but for her it was the most moving part of the service.

In other parts of the same parish, where the congregation was from a common-language background (ci-Bemba), listening and conversation took place in a different way. There would also be songs recently written and sung by the young choirs, and traditional hymns (translated from the English) that were loved by the older people – the elders. Both groups offered to God their deepest concerns in the ways most appropriate to themselves. Sometimes, one group within the church was critical of another either in the words of the songs or in the style of the music. For example, the young people would be critical of what they considered to be the hypocritical behaviour of their elders (this happens the world over), as can be seen in the following words of a song that they would sing. In this song, which warns of God's judgement, choir members also realize that they too will be judged:

> To all mankind, come and kneel before me.
> *Chorus*: We shall see Jesus and we shall say according to what we do.
> He will ask how each one worked. Some will say, 'I was a choir
>   member.' What about you, father, seated there? 'You are my God,
>   I was a priest.'
> What about you, mother, seated there? 'I, my Lord, I was a Mothers'
>   Union member.'
> And you, father, seated there? 'My Lord, I was a deacon.'

> He will come with his angels to catch his children. They have failed to
> teach, even though they have come from my house. Catch them and
> put them in the life prison.

It is traditional in Africa to express criticism through music and song. The congregation would be willing to listen to such songs, even though the criticism was levelled against them. After the service in which a song such as this was sung, there would usually be lively conversation! Here the church was a place of listening and conversation in a creative and natural way. Both young and old attended it because their voice was heard and valued.

Finally, sharing fears about coming to agreement requires an enormous amount of trust, and can be as challenging as real listening. Today's agreement can undermine yesterday's battles and sacrifices.

Taking Dr Daly's situation as an example, the warring factions in Northern Ireland discovering that they can live and work together can be viewed as insulting the memory and sacrifice of those who have given their lives for the struggle. The significance of memory and how we remember is an important issue. The fears about coming to agreement are as much related to the past as they may be to the present.

Archbishop Daly's model can be helpful at the intrapersonal as well as the personal, political and communal levels. How we function as human persons is as complex as intercommunal dynamics, but if there is a struggle within ourselves, how far are the disputing factions able to be in dialogue with each other, and what do we fear would be lost if there were some form of inner reconciliation?

In his story, Dr Daly is saying that it is important to journey to the other and back (for A to make a journey to B and vice versa) in order to see our common history from their viewpoint as well as ours, rather than bring down a barrier and insist on the absolute truth of our own perspective. We shall return to the crippling effect of fear, but first a fuller exploration of embracing the other is required.

There are a number of ways of embracing the other, but the one that appears to be prevalent in society is through dichotomy or opposition that brings with it a deep suspicion of the other. Perhaps embracing the other through dichotomy is best illustrated via the adversarial system of British politics. There is government and there is opposition. The role of the opposition is to oppose government. The organization of the House of Commons reflects and reinforces this style of communicating by not allowing opposing members of the House to cross certain lines that, when they were first painted, were just beyond the stretch of opposing swords. There are, of course, strengths in this form of governing, but recently leaders of major political parties have tried to move away from the blanket principle of opposing for the sake of opposing. In this political climate, which is a reflection of a particular philosophical approach, otherness, whether it be other ideas, other ideologies or other people, is embraced, but with reluctance and difficulty. On the one hand, a critical engagement with otherness is important and healthy, but on the other, an atmosphere can be created where an underlying fear will bring about rejection before a critical engagement can take place.

Another way of embracing the other is to see the other as a potential friend and ally rather than a potential enemy. The Jewish philosopher Martin Buber, who has had a wide influence on thinkers of many faiths, including many Christian theologians, articulated this in terms of an I–Thou relationship. Buber argues that human existence is shaped by the way in which we dialogue with each other, with the world and with God. Relating to another in the I–Thou relationship recognizes the unique value of the other person (the Thou), accepts the other as a fellow human being and is seeking a relationship of mutuality and reciprocity. When people are in dialogue with God (the only perfect Thou), the I–Thou relationship is sustainable. Buber contrasts the I–Thou, subject-to-subject relationship, with the I–It, subject-to-object relationship, which is characterized by separateness and detachment. In the I–It relationship, the other is not regarded with respect and dignity and can be regarded as less than human.

Yet another way of relating to the other is by embracing difference. The extent of love for the person who is closest to us can be seen in the way we allow them to be themselves so that they can grow into the person God has created them to be. That person may be very different from us in the way they think and act, and they may not end up just as we would choose for them to be – but it is important not to mix up love with control. In John Bayley's moving biography of his wife Iris Murdoch's decline into Alzheimer's disease, he describes their deepening relationship with the phrase that they grew 'closer and closer apart'. A relationship bound around with love respects the other even though it may not be easy. It gives gap and spaces in the relationship. Christian theology embodies this in the Trinity, where it is the respecting of the otherness of the three persons of the Trinity, Father, Son and Holy Spirit, that forms unity. Otherness is constitutive of unity; it does not come as a result of unity.

In his book, *The Dignity of Difference*, Chief Rabbi Jonathan Sachs, surveying the political and religious scenes, makes a plea for tolerance in an age of extremism. Today's fundamentalisms, Sachs argues, provide the biggest risks to the earth's survival, and he interprets the disaster of 9/11 as the clashing of the two fundamentalisms of global capitalism and an extremist form of Islam. When one group decides that all other ways of thinking and acting apart from its way are not legitimate or permissible, that group is on the way to promoting fundamentalism. In fundamentalist thinking, difference is heavily controlled to avoid diversity. The heart of his thesis in support of embracing difference is summed up in the prologue:

> Crises happen when we attempt to meet the challenges of today with the concepts of yesterday. That is why nothing less than a paradigm shift may be needed to prevent a global age becoming the scene of intermittent but destructive wars. I speak from within the Jewish tradition, but I believe that each of us from within our own traditions, religious or secular, must learn to listen and be prepared to be surprised by others. We must make ourselves open to their stories, which may profoundly conflict with ours. We must even, at times, be ready to hear of their pain, humiliation and resentment and discover that their image of us is anything but our image of ourselves. We must learn the art of conversation, from which truth emerges not, as in Socratic dialogues, by the refutation of falsehood but from the quite different process of letting our world be enlarged by the presence of others who think, act and interpret reality in ways radically different from our own. We must attend to the particular, not just the universal. For when universal civilizations clash, the world shakes, and lives are lost . . . God has created many cultures, civilizations and faiths but only one world in which to live together – and it is getting smaller all the time.[3]

Embracing the other is a risky enterprise. It requires a willingness to be vulnerable and open to change. Reconciliation will only be possible if a person, or a group, is willing to readjust their identity in the light of the otherness of the other. This does not mean going against one's principles (unless, after close examination, those principles are not built on reconciling foundations), nor does it mean losing one's identity. Or does it?

At some point in the process of embracing the other, fear, usually the fear of losing one's identity, will arise. Fear is one of the greatest enemies of the gospel, and it is liable to infiltrate our being at a time we least expect and feel least able to handle it. It may arise over fear of losing something large, but it may equally well up over what may appear to be the most petty of incidents.

On the positive side, fear can encourage caution to think and pray through an action with care. On the negative side, fear can be a trap that discourages innovation and prevents the approaching of new horizons. Jesus recognized this same fear when he told his followers that in order to gain life (a new identity) it was important to lose an old identity:

> If any want to become my followers, let them deny themselves and take up their cross and follow me. For those who want to save their life will lose it, and those who lose their life for my sake, and for the sake of the gospel, will save it. (Mark 8.34–35)

This does not mean losing all traces of the essence of our being to become a totally different person unknown even to ourselves, but rather it means a willingness to cast aside all those things that prevent us from becoming the person God has created us to be. So if this means shedding, or relegating to another part of the body, those parts that deny rather than promote reconciliation, then so be it. It is in embracing the other that this can happen.

Excluding the other

Ethnic cleansing, with its roots in a search for (false) purity and security, provides the worst examples of excluding and rejecting the other. Hutu against Tutsi in Rwanda, Serb against Bosnian in the Balkans and Aryan against Jew in Germany are some of the worst forms of ethnic cleansing in recent history, and they are all embodiments of the rejection of the other. Rejection of the other is not confined to history and there are many examples today nearer to home. Whenever a group of people's presence or ways of thinking pose a threat to the interests of the established group, whether that group be community, church or family, they may be identified as an 'enemy' and rejected. Of course, it is important for the established group to challenge and ask questions where appropriate, but the climate in which this is done is vitally important. Indeed, in order to grow as human beings, there needs to be competition as well as affirmation, but all competition and no affirmation are as inimical to growth as all affirmation and no competition. Christians need simultaneously to live in two worlds that are difficult to inhabit at the same time: to be people of conviction and at the same time open and vulnerable to new insights God is trying to provide. There needs to be a true spirit of listening, otherwise difference becomes division through exclusion of the other.

The tendency to exclusion is subversive. Even though people may boast of inclusive policies and attitudes, the shadow side, the irrepressible urge to exclude, is not far away. For example, many Western governments quite rightly place high value on human rights and equal opportunity agendas, championing the rights of minority groups, yet at the same time in their approach to other countries some regard all forms of culturally appropriate government by consent a threat unless they are Western-style democracies. The important point here is that while an enormous amount is owed to Western democracy, political otherness is regarded as unacceptable on the international scene. It is not uncommon for otherness to be embraced in one aspect of life only to be rejected in another.

Tendency to exclude is part of human nature – even the most enlightened of people have exclusionary tendencies. What is important is an awareness of them. It is a matter of particular concern when religious organizations use religious language to justify excluding the other. Jesus himself was constantly fighting against the way his community regarded social outcasts as sinners. There were certain groups, excluded from membership of Jewish religious society, whom Jesus sought out and affirmed. Tax collectors were referred to in the same breath as sinners – Jesus, to the consternation of the religious establishment, called down Zacchaeus from a tree and went to dinner with him (Luke 19.1–10). Samaritans were regarded with hostility – Jesus used Samaritans as examples of righteousness (Luke 10.29–37; 17.16). The story of the man born blind (John 9.1–41) illustrates the belief that the man is blind because of his sin (John 9.2, 34). Jesus challenged all these stereotypes and paid the price for his challenges, but what his example shows is the dangers faced by organizations of good people set up for good reasons. It is easy to point a finger at the religious authorities who were active in the crucifixion of Jesus and dismiss them as innately evil. There were certainly dark forces at work within their activities, but the majority of the people were undoubtedly good and pious people wanting to do the best for their beliefs. Are religious establishments any different today? Which are the groups being excluded today?

The tendency to exclude the other may also be subtle and done in a controlling way. Some forms of exclusion are presented as inclusion. Assimilation is a form of exclusion of the other in that it incorporates one group into the ways and customs of the dominant group, expecting them to conform. Assimilation is very much a live issue in Britain at present as the multi-cultural nature of society is high on the agenda. Assimilation says that you must become a clone of me, whereas those supporting the multi-cultural approach say that you and your people can live here keeping your own customs and traditions, provided there is no clash with our customs and traditions. Assimilation rejects your identity and otherness in order to achieve unity; multi-culturalism allows otherness and identity to continue and flourish but its proponents are not strong in articulating a vision that can be owned and debated by society as a whole. This is an important debate to be had, but the recent swing of the pendulum is worryingly close to assimilation where other cultural and religious identities are not respected. Assimilation can also be an issue in personal relations. It is possible in a relationship for the identity of one person to be subsumed into that of another. When love is confused with control, there is an exclusion of otherness.

Another form of exclusion is abandonment. It is possible simply to ignore deliberately a group or a person with whom there would normally be contact because to be in dialogue with them would be too costly. Such a group may be people crying out because of hunger and injustice in Africa, the travellers who have made an encampment in our community or a member of our family imprisoned for an unspeakable crime. This is well exemplified in the story of the Good Samaritan, where the priest and the Levite did not engage with the man who was beaten and left for dead, fearing that to do so would prevent them from carrying out their role as religious officials (Luke 10.29–37). There are many causes and people who jostle for our attention, and it is not possible to respond to all; but to turn away through fear of engaging with otherness is a form of exclusion.

It is possible to check whether the otherness of a person or group is being excluded by asking how far their otherness is being respected and how much space they are being given to become the people that God has created them to be.

Dehumanizing the other

An alcoholic was deeply moved by the support he was given by a Christian lady who was with him on his difficult journey from addiction. As part of his new way of life, he decided to attend his local church. When asked by the lady whether he felt at home in the church, he replied that they were kind and welcoming and everybody wanted to help him, but nobody wanted to be friends with him. He was regarded as a person with a problem rather than a human being in his own right – seeing him as somebody to be helped meant that people would not have to engage with the otherness of his personality. Before excluding a person or group from the world that we inhabit, we exclude them from the human race. Those whom we want to reject we dehumanize and even demonize by calling them such names as 'dirty', 'savages', 'terrorists', 'perverts', 'psychos'. By dehumanizing them, their otherness is being rejected.

The Musalaha organization under the care of Salim Munayer has already been mentioned in the Introduction. Reflecting on his experiences of working to reconcile Israeli and Palestinian young people, Salim has listed conduct that dehumanizes others. Although developed in the context of Israeli–Palestinian reconciliation, his findings can be applied elsewhere:

1 There is a division between 'us' and 'them'. People tend to evaluate their own group in a positive light but gloss over its shortcomings. Such an approach helps distinguish between 'us' (who are right and good) and 'them' (who are wrong and bad).

2 In dehumanization, the other is seen as an enemy. Thus, Palestinians will see Israelis as people who want to steal their land and remove them; Israelis will see Palestinians as terrorists wanting to push them into the sea.

3 There is a failure to see complexity on the other side. All of 'them' are the enemy and they all want to kill us. This approach fails to recognize that there are some on the other side who will be working for peace and reconciliation. It also fails to see the other as people created in the image of God.

4 There is a suspicion towards the other side, who are always considered to be acting with ulterior motives, especially when they do not behave in accordance with our mental picture of them. A conspiracy theory develops whereby the other is suspected of being up to no good.

5 A self-fulfilling prophecy evolves. The other will be provoked into behaving in accordance with the image that is projected upon them, and when they do we say, 'What did I tell you? I knew all

along they would behave like this.' Another element of this is that once there is division, we tend to remember our enemies as they were in the past and do not allow them to move on. There develops a certainty that the other only understands power, and so the language of communication is power and violence.

6 Each side develops a sense of moral superiority and views with contempt those who have other values. There is a fear of mixing with the other side because taking their moral values seriously by discussing them may undermine or challenge mine.

7 At some level or other both Israelis and Palestinians regard themselves as victims and are therefore unable to recognize that they are a threat to the other. If one side sees themselves as victims, then they cannot see themselves as victimizer, which makes them blind to the other's struggle, anguish and hopes. Their self understanding as the threatened and injured party justifies fear and hostility towards the other. Some politicians prey on these fears to promote their own political agenda.

8 Demonization takes place. Each side believes that God is with them and therefore the devil must be on the other side. Often, religious language is used to rationalize this deeply felt belief, which in turn becomes the justification for violence.[4]

All these mechanisms of keeping the reality of the other at bay are obstacles to working towards reconciliation.

Otherness and communion

We have already seen that otherness cannot stand on its own but needs to be set alongside a desire for communion.[5] Respecting otherness without relating it to community and communion will bring about chaos and anarchy. Boundaries are essential. If Christians are to be faithful to their calling, then the otherness and communion should try to mirror that which exists in God the Holy Trinity. It is not possible to do this anything like fully or perfectly, which is why reconciliation cannot fully be achieved in this life, but that is the goal towards which we dance and struggle. In God, otherness is part and parcel of unity rather than something that emerges from it. Otherness is not a threat to unity but unity is conditional upon otherness. There is frequently a struggle in holding otherness and unity in tension, but humanity will be the richer from this creative dialectic. A family is stronger if the members are given the space to develop into the people God has created them to be rather than into clones of the parents – to hold together family and otherness will certainly involve struggle. A leading Derry sculptor, Maurice Harron, made a moving sculpture of two men, each standing on his own plinth facing the other, with right hands straining to make contact. It is entitled *Hands across the Divide*, and stands in Carlisle Square, Derry, overlooking the Craigavon Bridge, which crosses the river Foyle. Unveiled in 1991, the sculpture shows Protestant and Catholic stretching out towards the otherness of the other but struggling to hold on to their own identity (see this book's cover and <http://cain.ulst.ac.uk/images/photos/derry/citywithout/statuesbr.htm>).

I end this chapter with a passage from a report of a World Council of Churches Conference on Faith and Order. The conference was held in Santiago de Compostela, Spain, in 1993, and had as its theme, 'Towards *koinonia* (communion) in faith, life and witness'. The passage coalesces a number of the themes of this chapter and helps move on to the final one, which draws together some threads of this discussion about reconciliation. The report uses the word *koinonia* for communion:

> The dynamic process of *koinonia* involves the recognition of the complementarity of human beings. As individuals and communities, we are confronted by the others in their otherness, e.g. theologically, ethnically, culturally. *Koinonia* requires respect for the other and a willingness to listen to the other and to seek to understand them. In this process of dialogue, where each is changed in the encounter, there takes place the appropriation of the stories of action, reaction and separation whereby each has defined himself or herself in opposition to the other. The search for establishing *koinonia* involves appropriating the pain and hurt of the other and, through a process of individual and collective repentance, forgiveness and renewal, taking responsibility for that suffering. Confrontation with the other, individually and collectively, is always a painful process, challenging as it does our own lifestyle, convictions, piety and way of thinking. The encounter with the other in the search to establish the *koinonia*, grounded in God's gift, calls for a *kenosis* – a self-giving and a self-emptying. Such a *kenosis* arouses fear of loss of identity and invites us to be vulnerable, yet such is no more than faithfulness to the ministry of vulnerability and death of Jesus as he sought to draw human beings

into communion with God and each other. He is the pattern and patron of reconciliation which leads to *koinonia*.[6]

For individual, quiet reflection

1 Look at Fra Angelico's painting *The Adoration of the Magi*. What does it say about otherness (see <www.nga.gov/fcgi-bin/timage_f? object=41581&image=6313&c=gg4>)? What does Maurice Harron's *Hands across the divide* say about otherness (see <http://cain.ulst. ac.uk/images/photos/derry/citywithout/statuesbr.htm>)?

2 What, in your experience, has been most rewarding about embracing otherness, and where has this impacted on your own life and relationships?

3 What would be your greatest fear in engaging in discussion about seeking unity and reconciliation among differing church traditions, and how far would a sense of loss be a factor?

4 Reflect upon examples of excluding and dehumanizing the other.

For discussion in groups

1 Discuss examples of difference becoming division through the rejection of the other.

2 Is your Church a *place of listening and conversation* (as distinct from having people who are good at listening)? How can it become more so?

3 Consider the nature of our Parliament, especially the House of Commons, with its adversarial approach. Is there a better way?

4 Do you expect newcomers and youngsters to be assimilated into your church community or are you prepared to live with any differences and value the gifts they might bring, even if they do not fit with your tradition?

Prayer

Eternal God, whose image lies in the hearts of all people,
We live among peoples whose ways are different from ours,
whose faiths are foreign to us,
whose tongues are unintelligible to us.
Help us to remember that you love all people with your great love,
that all religion is an attempt to respond to you,

that the yearnings of other hearts are much like our own and are known to you.

Help us to recognize you in the words of truth, the things of beauty, the actions of love about us.

We pray through Christ, who is a stranger to no one land more than another, and to every land no less than to another.

World Council of Churches,
Vancouver Assembly, 1983

5

God's gift to the world

———◆·◆·◆———

Orthodox Christian representations of the resurrection, to be found on icons and wall paintings, do not show Jesus emerging from the tomb but rather his descent to the realm of the dead. Orthodox artists know that they cannot depict the moment of resurrection, so instead they represent the effects of the resurrection. All Orthodox representations of the resurrection (known as the *Anastasis*) have the same theme, although there are variations in the ordering of the figures. Jesus, in the centre, is identified by a ring of light and he is trampling underfoot the gates of hell – in some icons smashed padlocks and chains are in evidence. In all the depictions, tombs have been broken open as a result of Jesus' conquering death. A lively depiction of the *Anastasis* is on the apse of the Chora church, Istanbul (www.greek-icons.org/jesus_christ/8-jesus-christ-resurrection.html or http://en.wikipedia.org/wiki/Image:Kariye_ic.jpg). There are a number of ancestral figures whom Jesus meets. Abel, murdered by his brother Cain, is holding a shepherd's crook. The two kings (identified by their crowns) are David and Solomon (who, being more senior in age, has a beard), and John the Baptist can be seen between the two kings. Jesus is grasping the hands of Adam and Eve, reuniting them both as they emerge from their tombs. Jesus frees them from the darkness and alienation of death and leads them into the new life and light that he brings at the resurrection. This is a powerful illustration of reconciliation: Jesus reuniting alienated humanity and drawing them into a bright and transforming presence with new possibilities.

Previous chapters have shown that the themes of memory, victimhood, forgiveness and otherness have to be taken into account in the search for reconciliation. There are other themes, but these are particularly significant. This chapter will highlight the reality that, for the Christian, reconciliation is God's gift. Christianity does not have a monopoly over reconciliation, but it does have distinctive experiences of reconciliation to share with the world. As such, reconciliation is a form of mission. Reconciliation will not come from a set of techniques (helpful as they may be), nor from a particular definition (tempting as that may be), but rather it will come from relationship. There is no blueprint for bringing about reconciliation because it depends upon the issues and context, but one aspect that will not change is the need for relationship: a relationship with Jesus Christ and a willingness to embrace those with whom we wish to be reconciled. Reconciliation cannot take place unless we really want it and are willing to put ourselves out for it. It is not difficult to think of high principled reasons for not being reconciled.

First, I will focus on reconciliation in the Bible and then look at the significance of the climate and context in which reconciliation takes place. Then, after the role of religion as a whole in reconciliation, examples of communities, or parables, of reconciliation will be related. Indeed, should not all Christian churches be communities of reconciliation? We will then examine the Eucharist as the sacrament of reconciliation. Finally, just as Jacob fought with God and left the encounter a changed man, so too one sign that we have really engaged with reconciliation is that we are changed – and the more we have changed, the more deeply have we engaged. So we shall look at the marks of reconciliation.

Scripture and reconciliation

The passage that distils a theological understanding of reconciliation is to be found in St Paul's second letter to the Corinthians (2 Corinthians 5.18–21). However, reconciliation is an underground river that flows throughout the whole of Scripture, occasionally bubbling up to the surface and identifying itself. The last book of the Bible concludes with a picture of the New Jerusalem, where the world and creation are reconciled to God:

> The angel showed me the river of the water of life, bright as crystal, flowing from the throne of God and of the Lamb through the middle of the street of the city. On either side of the river is the tree of life with its twelve kinds of fruit, producing its fruit each month; and the

leaves of the tree are for the healing of the nations. Nothing accursed will be found there any more. But the throne of God and of the lamb will be in it, and his servants will worship him; they will see his face, and his name will be on their foreheads. And there will be no more night; they need no light of lamp or sun, for the Lord God will be their light, and they will reign for ever and ever.

(Revelation 22.1–5)

Those who turn their back on God are not part of the New Jerusalem, but the gates are always open (Revelation 21.25), leaving the opportunity for all to turn towards God, providing a corrective to the way that the tree of the knowledge of good and evil, forbidden to Adam, gave an opportunity to turn away from God (Genesis 2.16–17).

The book of Genesis begins with creation as God planned it and then, during and after the Fall, Genesis charts the way in which men and women fell out of relationship with God, each other, themselves and creation.[1] In the story of the Fall, enmity – in many ways the very opposite of reconciliation – is first brought in when God says to the serpent, 'I will put enmity between you and the woman, and between your offspring and hers' (Genesis 3.15). Furthermore, a similar enmity is put between human beings and nature when God says to Adam:

Because you have listened to the voice of your wife, and have eaten of the tree about which I commanded you, 'You shall not eat of it', cursed is the ground because of you; in toil you shall eat of it all the days of your life; thorns and thistles it shall bring forth for you; and you shall eat the plants of the field.   (Genesis 3.17)

Next, man and woman are expelled from Paradise (Genesis 3.22–24). The downward slope now becomes even steeper. Up to now, man and woman have learnt how to fall out with each other, both have fallen out with God and the relationship with nature has become a chore. But there is more, and worse, to come.

In Genesis 4, we learn of enmity between two brothers – a theme that occurs frequently in Genesis – when Cain and Abel fall out and Cain, jealous of Abel, murders his brother (Genesis 4.8). Humanity has fallen out with God and the consequence is that men and women fall out with each other, sometimes with lethal consequences. Eventually, when God saw the dire state into which his creation had declined, he decided to put an end to it – but not to Noah, who had found favour with the Lord. In the story of the Flood, Noah and his family with the animals they had taken into the ark were saved while all other living creatures were destroyed (Genesis 7).

These stories are important for the theme of reconciliation because they show the ways in which creation fell out of relationship with its Creator and itself. However, the next part of the story marks what the biblical scholar Clare Amos calls the 'genesis of reconciliation'. After the waters had subsided, God made a covenant with all humanity and all living creatures:

> Then God said to Noah and to his sons with him, 'As for me, I am establishing my covenant with you and your descendants after you, and with every living creature that is with you, the birds, the domestic animals, and every animal of the earth with you, as many as came out of the ark. I establish my covenant with you, that never again shall all flesh be cut off by the waters of a flood, and never again shall there be a flood to destroy the earth . . . This is a sign of the covenant that I make between me and you and every living creature that is with you, for all future generations: I have set my bow in the clouds, and it shall be a sign of the covenant between me and the earth.'
>
> (Genesis 9.8–13)

God is stretching out to creation. He is wanting to establish a fresh relationship. God is offering reconciliation.

The call of Abraham (Abram) is God's initiative in reconciliation. He calls out men and women to be instruments of reconciliation and Abraham is the first in a long line that culminates in Jesus Christ. The Lord says to Abraham:

> I will bless you, and make your name great, so that you will be a blessing. I will bless those who bless you, and the one who curses you I will curse; and in you all the families of the earth shall be blessed.
>
> (Genesis 12.2–3)

Those who are called to work with God in reconciliation will be a blessing to those around. But the work will be costly and hazardous. Abraham had to leave behind the familiarity of the past – 'Now the

LORD said to Abram, "Go from your country and your kindred and your father's house to the land that I will show you"' (Genesis 12.1). He also had to be willing to sacrifice the future, as can be seen from one of the most disturbing passages in Scripture, when he was asked to give up the only child he shared with his beloved wife, Sarah – God said, 'Take your son, your only son Isaac, whom you love, and go to the land of Moriah, and offer him there as a burnt-offering on one of the mountains that I shall show you' (Genesis 22.2). As we shall see, Jesus too had to give up his past (he 'emptied himself') in order to undertake his task of reconciliation; similarly, the cross showed a willingness for him to give up his future.

The other two major sagas in Genesis, first Jacob and Esau and then Joseph and his brothers, revolve around the theme of reconciliation. The stories realistically draw attention to human frailty in working towards reconciliation. Space does not allow consideration of both stories, but a few comments on Jacob and Esau will illustrate the centrality of the theme in Genesis and provide some important insights into understanding reconciliation as a whole.

Even before they were born, trouble was brewing between the twins Esau and Jacob. They struggled within the womb of Rebekah (their mother) and the Lord told Rebekah:

> Two nations are in your womb, and two peoples born of you shall be divided; one shall be stronger than the other, the elder shall serve the younger. (Genesis 25.23)

When the twins were born, Esau was the first-born, but Jacob followed, gripping the heel of his brother – an action that added another indication of what was to come. Esau, returning famished from his hunting, asked Jacob for some of the food he had cooked: Jacob would give it only on condition that Esau gave to Jacob the rights due to him as the first-born son. Esau agreed. But perhaps the seal upon the deteriorating relations between the two brothers who had shared their mother's womb was when Jacob, with the help of Rebekah, tricked his father into giving him the blessing he had reserved for his brother Esau (Genesis 27.18–40). As a result, 'Esau hated Jacob because of the blessing with which his father had blessed him, and Esau said to himself, "The days of mourning for my father are approaching; then I will kill my brother Jacob"'

(Genesis 27.41). The relationship had reached rock bottom. Jacob fled in fear.

Jacob spent the best part of 20 years with his mother's brother Laban. Then, returning to Canaan, Jacob prepared for an encounter with Esau, who was now a powerful man. Jacob was fearful that Esau would kill him and his family because Jacob now acknowledged that he had wronged his brother. It may be that Esau gave away his birthright too glibly – but Jacob asked an unreasonable price for a bowl of soup. Jacob had also tricked his brother out of his rightful blessing. Jacob was wanting reconciliation, and at the same time recognized that his brother had every cause to be angry.

Before he met with his brother, Jacob sent ahead gifts to appease him, to get him on his side. Jacob then spent the night before his meeting in a vigil, when he struggled with God: 'and a man wrestled with him until daybreak' (Genesis 32.24). This was a defining moment in his life. When daybreak came, Jacob would not let his opponent go until he had blessed Jacob. Jacob was asked, '"What is your name?" And he said, "Jacob." Then the man said, "You shall no longer be called Jacob, but Israel, for you have striven with God and with humans, and have prevailed"' (Genesis 32.27–28).

This is Jacob struggling with God and his relationship with Esau. Jacob tells his antagonist his name, a name meaning 'supplanter' or 'heel grabber' that represents his past, and he is renamed Israel, which means 'the one who strives with God'. This is to be seen as a type of confession of his past deeds and the taking on of a new identity. Jacob has had an experience of transformation in which there is a close link between reconciliation with God and reconciliation with his brother Esau. This is alluded to in the meeting of Jacob and Esau when Jacob says, 'truly to see your face is like seeing the face of God – since you have received me with such favour' (Genesis 33.10). The depth of our reconciliation with others is determined by the depth of our reconciliation with God.

The meeting between Esau and Jacob is surprising and moving. Jacob (Israel) approaches his brother with gestures of great respect and honour, all of which remain important in the Middle East today. 'But Esau ran to meet him, and embraced him, and fell on his neck and kissed him, and they wept' (Genesis 33.4). Reconciliation was taking place. Jacob's comment that seeing the face of Esau is like seeing the face of God is a reminder that for reconciliation to take place, it is essential that we see the image of God in the person with whom we are seeking reconciliation. Furthermore, it requires the image of God within us to recognize the same in the other. Without these two realities, reconciliation is simply not possible. Many see the story of Jacob (Israel) and Esau reflecting the contemporary story between Israeli and Arab (Palestinian). Also within the story of Jacob (Israel) and Esau lay possibilities for reconciliation for their modern-day descendants.

The reason for spending so much time at the beginning of the Bible is to show that reconciliation is deeply embedded in Scripture. Also, throughout the book, the New Testament has been extensively drawn upon to illustrate themes of reconciliation and it is important to redress the balance. God's attempts at reconciliation began with Abraham, and the journey can be traced through the patriarchs and prophets. But God is dealing with human beings with their strengths and weaknesses, and those whom God calls to be reconcilers on his behalf, such as Jacob, have themselves to be reconciled with others and with God himself. It is now time to turn to the New Testament, where reconciliation is embodied in Jesus Christ.

Although the Greek words for reconciliation only appear 15 times in the New Testament and nearly always in Paul's letters, reconciliation is the air breathed by the New Testament authors. We have considered at length the story of the All-loving Father in Luke (15.11–32), where forgiveness leads to reconciliation. St John's Gospel highlights that God's love for the world, embodied in Jesus Christ, is the basis for reconciliation (John 3.16–17). In the Sermon on the Mount, Jesus lists the qualities that make for reconciliation (Matthew 5). In the same passage, St Matthew points to the close connection between reconciliation with God and with neighbour:

> So when you are offering your gift at the altar, if you remember that your brother or sister has something against you, leave your gift before the altar and go; first be reconciled to your brother or sister, and then come and offer your gift.　　(Matthew 5.23–24)

But it is St Paul who places his finger on the theme and focuses its true meaning and significance. Paul's whole life was a struggle for reconciliation. Paul struggled for reconciliation with God (Acts 9), within himself (Romans 7.14–21) and with others (1 Corinthians 1.10–17), and he sees creation as part of the movement (Romans 8.19). It is not surprising, therefore, that reconciliation is central to his thinking and theology.

Indeed, one of Paul's greatest passages highlights reconciliation in the context of his own rejection by the Christian community in Corinth, which suspected his motives and questioned his authority to teach. Paul speaks about reconciliation in order to bring about reconciliation. It is highly charged and personal:

> So if anyone is in Christ, there is a new creation: everything old has passed away; see, everything has become new! All this is from God, who reconciled us to himself through Christ, and has given us the ministry of reconciliation; that is, in Christ God was reconciling the world to himself, not counting their trespasses against them, and entrusting the message of reconciliation to us. So we are ambassadors for Christ, since God is making his appeal through us; we entreat you on behalf of Christ, be reconciled to God.
>
> (2 Corinthians 5.17–20)

Again, reconciliation to God is at the heart of all forms of reconciliation, and God has reconciled humanity to himself through Jesus Christ. This is a new way of relating ('everything has become new') brought by God. Previously, God related to humanity through the Law, but now God relates to humanity through Jesus Christ. But there is more. Paul is telling the Corinthian church that they have a ministry of reconciliation ('has given us the ministry of reconciliation') and our effectiveness as followers of Jesus Christ will be judged by how seriously we act on this ministry of reconciliation ('So we are ambassadors for Christ, since God is making his appeal through us').

For Paul, God is the one who initiates and brings reconciliation. It is God's gift. What is also significant, and distinctive, is that God brings reconciliation even though he is the one who has been wronged or offended. In many cultures, there is an understanding that the person who has caused the rift should take steps to repair it. Acknowledgement of fault is a precondition to reconciliation. But – and this has already been demonstrated – this is not the case for Christians:

For if while we were enemies, we were reconciled to God through the death of his Son, much more surely, having been reconciled, will we be saved by his life. But more than that, we even boast in God through our Lord Jesus Christ, through whom we have now received reconciliation. (Romans 5.10–11)

Finally, Paul writes about reconciliation in a much less personal way in his letter to the Colossians where the apostle is alerting the church to false teachings. Here, reconciliation is shown to have cosmic dimensions, linking together creation and redemption:

For in him [Christ] all the fullness of God was pleased to dwell, and through him God was pleased to reconcile to himself all things, whether on earth or in heaven, by making peace through the blood of the cross. (Colossians 1.19–20)

Climate and context of reconciliation

Although reconciliation will take different forms in different contexts, the climate in which it is being sought needs to be the same, whatever the context. Noah Salameh is the founder of the Centre for Conflict Resolution and Reconciliation (CCRR) in Bethlehem. CCRR has two main objectives: first, to bring about peace 'from the inside', that is, peace between people and families and communities; second, to bring about reconciliation. In order for this to happen, Noah and his workers set about creating an atmosphere in which different groups can meet and be open with each other in order to talk about reconciliation. For example, he has brought together journalists from Israel and Palestine, members of the security forces from both sides, and teachers.

Noah is concerned to work from the 'bottom up', that is, to involve the ordinary people on the ground rather than encourage an industry of academic paper-writing that may have little or no effect outside academe. To this end, his field workers are active in schools and in the community in general. It is costly, because as a Palestinian Muslim, he is often accused of compromising with the forces of occupation. However, he is not deflected for long from his aim of ensuring that people have a climate in which they are able to talk openly and honestly. Unless the climate is right, conversations about reconciliation cannot take place. On a visit to a speaking engagement at a school, the teachers immediately attacked what he was trying to do. Noah challenged them by saying he had not received the welcome that he, as a visitor, would expect to receive, and that they had not respected his presence by listening to him. Such customs are particularly important in the Middle East. The teachers apologized to him. Once the need for civility had been established, good and fruitful conversation took place.

In situations of conflict, the first casualties are often the customs and civilities that are the glue of all cultures and families. Whether one is working for reconciliation between individuals, families or nations, it is essential that there be a climate where those involved can speak with openness and honesty. Reconciliation cannot be pursued in an environment of hostility and fear.

The processes for working towards reconciliation vary with the context and culture. In a number of cultures (for example African and Arabic), the community and its leaders play a significant role in the reconciliation of two people or their families, whereas in the West it is a much more private affair with a mediator. In Lebanon, remaining silent when another person speaks can be interpreted as agreement – there is an expectation to interrupt; in the West, it is regarded as rude to interrupt. In the West, a mediator is expected to be neutral, often drawn in from outside; in Arab–Islamic culture, the mediator would be an unbiased insider of some standing in the community who has a relationship with those in dispute.

The main purpose of this book is to examine reconciliation from a Christian perspective, but that is not the most common understanding. Political reconciliation is more akin to accommodation, usually agreeing the lowest possible threshold with which all parties can co-exist. Recent flare-ups in the Balkan states following the settlements in the 1990s raise questions about the processes and depth of reconciliation achieved. Deep-seated grievances were left to fester. For Jordanian Bedouin tribes, *suhl* is the customary process of settlement, where reconciliation (*musalaha*) is regarded as the best of judgements. Once a settlement has been agreed, there is handshaking (*mustafa*) and the sharing of bread and salt (*mumalaha*). Even though 'the best of judgements' is agreed between communities, it is not unknown for hostility to be buried only to flare up in a more virulent form years later.

The role of religion

In a lecture in Westminster Cathedral in April 2008, former Prime Minister Tony Blair highlighted the work of his Faith Foundation, to be launched the following month, and argued that religion needed to be rescued from extremism and irrelevance to help meet a 'profound yearning within the human spirit' at a time of unprecedented global turbulence. He intends that his Foundation will help 'partner those within any of the faiths who stand up for peaceful co-existence and reject the extremist and divisive notion that faiths are in fundamental struggle against each other'.

Since September 11, 2001 there has been a recognition by the majority that religion and faith have a significant role to play on the world's stage. Sadly, religion has provided divine ratification for many atrocities. The trials of those whose intention was to kill and maim in the summer of 2006 on flights to the USA, as well as those convicted of the bombings in London in July 2005, have shown the misuse of religion at its worst. On the other hand, religion has also provided the climate and language of reconciliation as religious leaders continued a dialogue in the background while political leaders strutted their stuff on the world stage.

Not only is it important that religion and faith are involved in such dialogues, they need to be reconciled between themselves. At one time there was an ecumenical imperative for churches to be in dialogue, and one of the reasons for the formation of the World Council of Churches was to promote it. Now there is a *world* imperative for faiths to be in dialogue. St John reminds us that Christians need to be one, 'so that the world may believe' (John 17.21). Today it is becoming increasingly apparent that faiths need to be in dialogue so that the world may survive.

The challenge for the twenty-first century is to provide environments and climates in which dialogue can take place between the major faiths and religions, where each acknowledges the 'otherness' of the 'other'. In such a dialogue each needs to be true to itself, holding firm to beliefs that are essential to the integrity of the faith. So for Christianity it is important not to compromise on its mission to witness to the liberating good news of God's love, embodied fully in the life, death and resurrection of Jesus Christ, while at the same time being open to dialogue.

Parables of reconciliation

The Church is called to be a parable of reconciliation. It is called to embody reconciliation in its own life and to be an agent of reconciliation. Its vocation is to make God's gift of reconciliation available to the world. There are many forms of reconciliation, but the gift offered by God is rich and distinctive as well as costly and transformative. While all churches should strive to be embodiments of reconciliation, some Christian communities have made it a particular emphasis in their mission.

The International Centre for Reconciliation (ICR) is based at Coventry Cathedral. Its roots date back to the Second World War. After the medieval cathedral was bombed by the Germans in 1940, a local priest was walking through the smouldering ruins and, finding three nails from the destroyed beams, tied them together with wire in the shape of a cross. This Cross of Nails has become a symbol of reconciliation, recognized throughout the world. Shortly after, the Provost asked the cathedral's stonemason to make an altar from the rubble and to place behind it a cross made from two charred beams that had fallen from the roof. The Cross of Nails was placed on the altar of rubble and the Provost had the words 'Father forgive' inscribed on the wall behind the altar. Not 'Father forgive *them*' but 'Father forgive', because he recognized the futility of war and knew that *all* involved in war have some level of responsibility. Furthermore, the Provost gathered as many nails as he could find, had them made into crosses and sent them to heads of state and spiritual leaders throughout the world as symbols of peace. Through these acts, he was signalling in a powerful and symbolic way that the response to war should be reconciliation rather than revenge, and the ICR has continued this work. Since then, it has worked for peace in some of the most troubled areas in the world and coordinates the community of the Cross of Nails, which undergirds the ICR with a spiritual and practical support base.

In 1993, a massive IRA bomb destroyed St Ethelburga's Church, and much of the surrounding area, in the City of London. After it was discovered that, despite the damage, the church could be repaired, it was decided that the best response to the bombing was to restore the building, making it a centre for reconciliation and peace with a special concern for the religious aspect of conflict and the role played by faith in its resolution. In 2002, the restored church was reconsecrated and the centre opened. One creative innovation at St Ethelburga's is the 'Tent'. Made of goat's hair in the Middle East, the Bedouin-style Tent has been erected behind the church and is used as a meeting place where people of different faiths convene to explore differences and build foundations for future collaboration. Entering the Tent, you have to remove your shoes as you stand in a sacred space – the rugs on the ground have been woven in places of conflict across the world. This is a place where peacemakers from across the world come to reflect on their experiences and an arena for all interested in exploring reconciliation locally, nationally and internationally, within themselves and within their faith.

These are two examples of the Church focusing on the role of re-conciliation. But there are many more, such as Corrymeela, an ecumenical Christian Community established in 1965 to promote reconciliation and peace in Northern Ireland, and Sant'Egidio in Rome, founded by a high-school student in 1968 to put the gospel into practice, especially in the service of reconciliation. To this end, members of the community of Sant'Egidio have been mediators in conflicts in Guatemala and Mozambique. Their work in reconcili-ation has frequently grabbed the headlines, but the community is concerned that the importance of prayer both in the community and in their work of reconciliation is not overlooked.

Indeed, the final example of a remarkable community of reconcili-ation is known primarily for prayer and worship being at the heart of all that it is. Nestling in the Burgundy hills of France is the tiny village of Taizé. It is here, not far from the ancient monastery of Cluny, that a spiritual revolution has taken place. The foundations of what was to become the ecumenical community of Taizé started some years before, but it was in 1949 when seven brothers committed themselves to lifelong vows of celibacy and great simplicity of life. 'The Lord Christ, in his compassion and his love for you, has chosen you to be in the church a sign of brotherly love. It is his will that with your brothers you live the parable of community' – these are words spoken during the life commitment of a brother in the community. The 'parable of community' set out to give concrete expression to re-conciliation. Brother Roger, founder of the community, wrote:

In my youth I was astonished to see Christians, whose lives are after all rooted in a God of love, using so much energy in justifying the divisions. So I said to myself that it was essential to create a community with a small number of men, but men who had decided to give their entire lives. A community where we would seek always to understand each other and to be reconciled, with goodness of heart and simplicity, would be at the centre of everything. To accomplish together the everyday, concrete step of being reconciled, day by day, and by doing this to make a little parable of Communion visible. To give reconciliation concrete expression in everyday life. To make it a reality without delay.[2]

Brother Roger was anxious to enable new possibilities of healing the deep divisions within the Church, and he found his Christian identity by choosing the path of reconciling within himself the Protestant faith of his origins with the mysteries of the Catholic faith, delighted that he could walk this path without falling out of communion with anybody. The pursuit of reconciliation is reflected in the community itself, which is made up of around one hundred brothers from Catholic and Protestant churches. The wellspring of Brother Roger's passion and commitment was his search for a life of communion with God. He believed that a relationship with God was in the depths of every human being: 'Communion with the living God touches what is unique and most intimate in the depths of the being.'[3] For him it was a constant *search* for communion with God, embodied in a parable of community that was itself seeking to embody reconciliation. His approach was a testimony to the understanding that the unity of the Church and the unity of the world are intimately related.

From the early 1960s, young adults came to Taizé in ever-increasing numbers to share in the prayer of the community and to be listened to by the brothers. They saw in the community a group of brothers who authentically lived the search for reconciliation, and the young people wanted to be part of the search. Brother Roger's main aim was to encourage young people to promote peace and reconciliation in the places where they live. Today, after Brother Roger's violent death, the Community is as vibrant as ever and continues in its mission.

Taizé is an important story in reconciliation because it reminds us, perhaps more than any other, that the heart of reconciliation lies in the heart of God. It also makes clear that reconciliation is a joyful act of liberation. The writings of Brother Roger and the songs of Taizé overflow with themes that liberate for reconciliation. Here are three of those themes.

1 Joy is important. Brother Roger writes, 'God wants us to be happy. It is up to us to detect the gospel realities that make life beautiful: trust, the spirit of praise, an overflowing heart, a joy renewed at every moment.'
2 It is important to know that God forgives us. Brother Roger writes, 'By forgiving us, God buries our past in the heart of Christ and brings relief to the secret wounds of our being.'
3 Love is at the heart of it all. Again, Brother Roger writes, ' "Love and say it with your life," said St Augustine. Without a love that forgives, without reconciliation, what future is possible for human beings?'[4]

Taizé is important in the story of reconciliation because it provides deep spiritual foundations and a reminder that, for Christians, reconciliation lies at the heart of a relationship with God, where love, joy and forgiveness figure highly.

Not every local church can be a Taizé or a St Ethelburga's, but every church, in its own way, is called to be a parable of reconciliation that tries to embody reconciliation in its life and in its witness.

The sacrament of reconciliation

If reconciliation looks for repentance on the side of the guilty, so too it looks to those who are wronged to give up a sense of righteousness over and against the guilty. Therapists argue that there is no evidence that the distress of a painful memory is relieved by dwelling on the guilt of the perpetrator. Truth, honesty and justice are important, but at some point the process of forgiveness needs to begin otherwise all parties will be locked and unable to move and reconciliation will be an impossibility. Recognizing the Eucharist as the sacrament of reconciliation and the very place where the gift of reconciliation is handed to us can help with this.

At the Eucharist we remember before God the wrongs done against us. We will, quite understandably, want God to comfort us in our pain and may express anger against those who have committed the wrong, or we may even express anger against God himself. While we are traumatized by the wrong done to us, there may be nothing more that we can do. However, as pointed out in Chapter 1, if I only remember before God the wrong done to me, then I will be sacralizing the way I am using my memory, which may also be condemning the person who has wronged me. But the God who comforts us in our pain and distress also removes the guilt of transgressors. From the cross Jesus cried for the forgiveness of those who were crucifying him. A Christian community that prays for those who have been wronged and, like Jesus on the cross, prays for God's forgiveness for the perpetrators of evil, would change the world. This does not run away from the wrongs that have been committed, but remembers them in a way that does not feed feelings of hatred. Bishop Leonard Wilson did this by seeing his tormentors not as they were but as they had been. (See Chapter 3, p. 61.) Through the grace of God, it may also be possible to see them as they could be.

The Christ being received at the Eucharist through word and sacrament is the Christ who both suffered unjustly and forgave his tormentors from the cross. When Christ is received in this way, the worshipper is transcending his or her humanity and becoming God's new creation, who can love wrongdoers regardless of what they have done, thereby being freed from the hold of the wrong suffered, and can also stretch out a hand of reconciliation to the one who has inflicted the wrong. It is impossible for human beings to do this in their own strength, but only with God's help.

Marks of reconciliation

Memory, victimhood, forgiveness and otherness are features that always figure in reconciliation. In addition, reconciliation will not have happened unless all parties in the process are open to the fact that involvement will mean fresh understandings, transformation, opposition and cost.

Fresh understandings

Reconciliation requires a willingness to cross thresholds that have solidified into 'precious' differences. Such a willingness will result in an enlarged understanding of oneself, the world and God. The dismantling of apartheid required at least some white South Africans to believe that men and women are equal before God and the law, regardless of the colour of their skin. In the early Church, the apostles were vexed by the question of whether non-Jews who wanted to become followers of Christ, himself a Jew, should be circumcised. Some argued that unless followers were circumcised according to the custom of Moses, then they could not be saved, whereas others believed that God has already been working through uncircumcised Gentiles and that circumcision should not be required for them to be welcomed into the Church. An account of this dispute can be found in Acts 15, in verses that hint at the vehemence and depth of feeling of a debate that could have torn the young Church apart. In the end, it was decided that circumcision would not be required, but Gentiles would be told to abstain from certain pagan practices (Acts 15.13–21). This was a defining moment in the life of the Church; it provided a fresh and broader understanding of what it meant to be a follower of Christ.

The Church has faced similar defining moments throughout its history and it will continue to do so. Often theological disputes supply the arena in which political differences are played out, and the outcome will depend upon the willingness of the protagonists to move forward together. It will also require people who can see God at work, beckoning them beyond the particular issues that define the dispute into a deeper relationship with God.

Another dispute that wracked the Church was the nature of Christ. Christians in the early Church were asking how he was related to God. Was he God or was he a man? If he were fully God, how could he be fully human? It was impossible, argued many, for Christ to be both. The debate intensified as the years went on, and men and women were defined as Christians by the stance they took on this particular debate. Some argued so hard for Christ being a human being that they had to concede that as Son he was not God in the same way as the Father. Others argued the opposite. They were absolutely resolute that Jesus was God in the same way as the Father, but they had to agree that he was not as human as the rest of us, which raised questions about how and whether he really suffered and died. The great Church Councils of Nicaea (in 325) and Chalcedon (in 451) were remarkable for what they achieved in addressing the disagreements over the nature of Christ. Of course, like all Church Councils, they had their share of infighting, backbiting, intrigue and political manoeuvrings, but between them they secured two great achievements. First, they made statements that marked out the boundaries of Christian belief – and Christians still recite them today. Second, they took the two positions about Jesus Christ being fully God or fully human and declared that he was both. Although not everybody could agree with the definitions that emerged (and the same is true today), two apparently irreconcilable views *were* reconciled, thereby embracing difference rather than narrowing possibilities. From the midst of the struggle, a fresh understanding of the nature of Christ was born.

Of course, there are occasions when one of the parties is wrong; and there can be no compromise with evil. Reconciliation should not be brought into the equation until the evil has ceased, the battle has subsided and all parties regard themselves as standing on an equal footing. When reconciliation does take place even in these circumstances, fresh understandings on all sides will be indicators of its effectiveness.

Transformation

Reconciliation cannot take place without transformation. Reflecting on the situation in South Africa, Desmond Tutu writes:

> In South Africa, the whole process of reconciliation has been placed in very considerable jeopardy by the enormous disparities between the rich, mainly the whites, and the poor, mainly the blacks. The huge gap between the haves and the have-nots, which was largely created and maintained by racism and apartheid, poses the greatest threat to reconciliation and stability in our country . . . That is why I have exhorted whites to be keen to see transformation taking place in the lot of blacks. Unless houses replace the hovels and shacks in which most blacks live; unless blacks gain access to clean water, electricity, affordable health care, decent education, good jobs and a safe environment – all things which the vast majority of whites have taken for granted for so long – we can kiss goodbye to reconciliation.[5]

For the situation of the blacks to be transformed, whites need to support transformation for blacks, which will be at some cost to whites. White South Africans need to view black South Africans not as terrorists but as human beings who have a right to share the country with them. Black South Africans need to view white South Africans as neighbours and equals. Our view of a person and of history has to be changed and transformed, which will affect our view of ourselves and of God.

In order for the planet to survive, human beings need to be reconciled with the environment. Humanity's attitude to nature will require a transformation of lifestyle. There will need to be a careful scrutiny of habits of consumption, which will need to be in dialogue with preservation and conservation. The arguments for a radical rethink of our relation with creation quite rightly bombard the media. What this all points to is the need to transform attitudes and habits towards nature.

For the Christian, transformation happens all around. At the resurrection, disaster is transformed to triumph: death is transformed from a millstone to a stepping stone. At the Eucharist, bread and wine is transformed into the body and blood of Christ. For this to be real, what happens in liturgy and story needs to be reflected in human relationships. Perhaps the biggest challenge is to bring about political transformation. How far is it possible to cross that often huge chasm between the Christian vision of reconciliation and the realities that confront us on the social and political stage? Gabriel Daly, an Augustinian priest, puts it succinctly when he writes:

> The will to reconciliation may begin as a desire to end hostilities or make the neighbourhood safer, and as such it is enormously important and beneficial. The task of the Christian, however, is to extend the process inwards into the hearts of men and women where it ceases to be 'mere business' and becomes an exercise in bringing about the Kingdom of God.[6]

Opposition

As noted in Chapter 1, the Church of the Resurrection in Jerusalem embraces the location of Jesus' crucifixion and resurrection – the very places where reconciliation brought about by God can be pinpointed. However, move only a short distance from here and one discovers the very opposite of reconciliation. The church itself is a bastion of dispute. Five Christian denominations claim ownership of this most sacred spot in Christendom, jealously guarding their patches of ground and duties. It is not uncommon for disputes and fights to break out within the church itself over some apparently petty squabble about responsibility for a particular task. This poor advertisement for Christian unity becomes even less convincing when one recalls that because Christians could not agree about ownership of this place of reconciliation, the key to the door is held by a Muslim family. But it gets worse when one realizes that this place of reconciliation is located in a most divided region of the world that feeds some of the worst violence on the planet.

Reconciliation provokes enmity. The activity of reconciliation with its inherent requirement for transformation and change arouses the ire of those who stand to lose. The loss may be personal, political or financial. For one person reconciliation may include a loss of face, for another it may be a loss of position and for another a loss of investment. For the person who is trying to order their own inner life, it may be loss of security as he or she is challenged to live life differently. Reconciliation always provokes opposition and enmity at some level.

The cost of reconciliation

Just as reconciliation provokes opposition and enmity, so too is it costly to all involved in the process. Desmond Tutu warns against 'cheap' reconciliation when he argues:

> Often there have been those who wanted to provide a spurious kind of reconciliation . . . a crying of 'Peace, peace,' where there is no peace, a daubing of the wall with whitewash, a papering over of the cracks instead of dealing with the situation as it demands, seriously facing up to the unpleasantness of it all. In South Africa, we have often heard people speaking disapprovingly of what they have called 'confrontation,' which they then opposed to 'reconciliation.' In this way . . . glorious gospel words have fallen into disrepute and have been horribly devalued so that many have come to think that 'reconciliation' meant making peace with evil, immorality, injustice, oppression and viciousness of which they are the victims and, quite rightly, they have rejected such a travesty of the genuine article. How could anyone really think that true reconciliation could avoid a proper consultation?[7]

Reconciliation requires all those involved to face up to harsh realities, itself a costly exercise, and is not helped by turning a blind eye to wrong. It requires an honest facing up to the awfulness and the humiliation.

Involvement will also take its toll on the reconcilers. Members of the South African Truth and Reconciliation Commission had a mental health worker to support them in their work of hearing events of almost unbearable pain. The mental health worker suggested ways they might look after themselves during their work, but nevertheless the stress took members to breaking point and beyond. One Commissioner's marriage broke down; many had disturbed sleep patterns; some became short tempered and quarrelsome and others were drinking far more than they should.

As a reconciler one becomes part of the problem in order to be part of the solution. No matter how impartial a reconciler tries to be, it is not possible to be totally objective. Indeed, it would not be helpful to be totally objective as it is important to identify with all parties of the dispute at some level in order to empathize with their position. For this reason, it is not uncommon for a reconciler to be accused of taking one side or the other. For Jesus Christ the cost of being a reconciler was the cross.

Christianity and reconciliation

I have deliberately resisted defining reconciliation because there is no universal definition. But the Christian faith has an important and distinctive contribution to make to reconciliation, not simply within the individual Christian but for communities, society, politics and creation. For Christians, reconciliation is based not on a set of techniques but upon relationship, stemming from a relationship with Jesus Christ who is God's embodiment of reconciliation. This reconciliation is available to individuals and communities: to one and all. Fed by God's love, joy and forgiveness, reconciliation can be recognized by certain marks – the fact that always emerging from it will be fresh understandings, it will involve transformation, it will provoke opposition and it will be costly.

The events of Good Friday are the climax of God's work of reconciliation – the Orthodox representation of the resurrection shows the work of reconciliation continuing. The human soul cries out for reconciliation, and this God-given cry, which starts within, reverberates around the whole of creation. It is gathered on the cross in the heart of Jesus Christ, God's gift to the world.

For quiet, individual reflection

1 Spend some time (at least five minutes) in silence looking at the resurrection from the church of the Chora. Consider what emerged from your silence. (See <www.greek-icons.org/jesus_christ/8-jesus-christ-resurrection.html> or <http://en.wikipedia.org/wiki/Image:Kariye_ic.jpg>.)

2 In what ways does your local church try to be a parable of reconciliation?

3 Have you been involved in reconciliation, either as a party being reconciled or as a reconciler? If so, have you experienced the marks of reconciliation?

For group discussion

1 What does the story of Jacob and Esau teach us about reconciliation? Does it speak to any contemporary political struggle today?

2 How do the events of Holy Week and Easter enrich your understanding of reconciliation, especially when you think of particular disputes or people needing reconciliation?

3 In what practical ways can you and your local community bring about reconciliation with creation?

Prayer

Almighty God, who called your Church to bear witness that you were in Christ reconciling the world to yourself: help us to proclaim the good news of your love, that all who hear it may be drawn to you; through him who was lifted up on the cross, and reigns with you in the unity of the Holy Spirit, one God, now and for ever.

Thirteenth Sunday after Trinity
Common Worship

Notes

———•◆•———

Introduction

1 Miroslav Volf, *Exclusion and Embrace*, Nashville, Abingdon Press, 1996, p. 29.

2 Rowan Williams, 'The Suspicion of Suspicion: Wittgenstein and Bonhoeffer', in Richard H. Bell (ed.), *The Grammar of the Heart*, San Francisco, Harper & Row, 1988 (p. 44); quoted from John De Gruchy, *Reconciliation – Restoring Justice*, London, SCM, 2002, p. 161.

1 Memory . . . or remembering

1 John Bayley, *Iris – A Memoir of Iris Murdoch*, London, Abacus, 1999, pp. 53–4.

2 Muhyi al-Din Ibn al-Zaki, 9 October, 1187, quoted in Mariam Shahin, *Palestine – A Guide*, Massachusetts, Interlink, 2005, p. 303.

3 A. B. Yehoshua, *The Wall and the Mountain*, Tel-Aviv, Zemorah-Bitan, 1989.

4 Nelson Mandela, *Long Walk to Freedom*, Randburg, South Africa, Macdonald Purnell, 1994, p. 617.

5 W. Brueggemann, *Hopeful Imagination*, Philadelphia, Fortress, 1986, pp. 128–9.

6 A. Schmemann, *The Eucharist: Sacrament of the Kingdom*, Crestwood, St Vladimir's Seminary Press, 1988 (p. 130); quoted in M. Volf, *The End of Memory*, Grand Rapids, Eerdmans, 2006.

2 Victimhood . . . or not

1 Some would argue that humans were the first sacrificial victims and animals later replaced them. See James G. Williams (ed.), *The Girard Reader*, New York, Herder & Herder, 2004, p. 292.

2 See <http://commons.wikimedia.org/wiki/Image:Francisco_de_ Zurbar%C3%A1n_006.jpg>.

3 Words © Michael Saward/Administered by the Jubilate Group, 4 Thorne Park Road, Torquay TQ2 6RX, UK <copyrightmanager@ jubilate.co.uk>. USED BY PERMISSION.

4 Ottobah Cugoano in Grenada, 1788, quoted in Stephen Tomkins, *William Wilberforce – a Biography*, Oxford, Lion, 2007, p. 120.

5 Nelson Mandela, *Long Walk to Freedom*, Randburg, South Africa, Macdonald Purnell, 1994, p. 511.

6 Quoted in K. Cragg, *Palestine: The Prize and Price of Zion*, London, Cassell, 1997, p. 89.

7 K. Cragg, *Palestine*, p. 90.

3 Forgiveness

1 For a fuller account, see Geiko Müller-Fahrenholz, 'Shame and Hurt', in A. Falconer and J. Liechty (eds), *Reconciling Memories*, Dublin, Columba Press, 1998, p. 237.

2 Quoted in G. Daly, 'Forgiveness and Community', in Falconer and Liechty, *Reconciling Memories*, p. 205.

3 M. Volf, *Exclusion and Embrace*, Nashville, Abingdon Press, 1996, p. 9.

4 Volf, *Exclusion and Embrace*, p. 163.

5 Volf, *Exclusion and Embrace*, p. 165.

6 Taken from <http://en.wikipedia.org/wiki/Gordon_Wilson_(peace_campaigner)>.

7 Quoted in Donald W. Shriver Jr, 'A Struggle for Justice and Reconciliation', in Falconer and Liechty, *Reconciling Memories*, p. 230.

8 See full text at <www.ttc.edu.sg/csca/rart_doc/ang/sing/wilson1946.htm>.

9 Quoted in S. Plant, 'How can there be forgiveness without remorse?', *The Times*, 25 August, 2007.

10 Quoted in H. Arendt, *The Human Condition*, Chicago, University of Chicago Press, 1998, pp. 238–9.

11 See John W. De Gruchy, *Reconciliation – Restoring Justice*, London, SCM, 2002, pp. 158–9.

12 Quoted in G. Daly, 'Forgiveness and Community', in Falconer and Liechty, *Reconciling Memories*, p. 204.

13 G. and M. Harcourt, *Short Prayers for the Long Day*, London, Collins, 1978, p. 104.

4 Reaching out to the other

1 See <www.nga.gov/fcgi-bin/timage_f?object=41581&image=6313&c=gg4>.

2 Carl R. Rogers, *On Becoming a Person*, Boston, Houghton Mifflin, 1961, p. 333.

3 J. Sachs, *The Dignity of Difference*, London, Continuum, 2002, p. 23.

4 Salim J. Munayer, 'On the Road to Reconciliation,' in Salim Munayer (ed.), *In the Footsteps of our Father Abraham*, Jerusalem, Musalaha, 2002, pp. 84–6.

5 I am indebted to the insights of John D. Zizioulas, *Communion and Otherness*, London, T&T Clark, 2006.

6 Quoted in Alan D. Falconer, 'The Reconciling Power of Forgiveness', in A. Falconer and J. Liechty (eds), *Reconciling Memories*, Dublin, Columba Press, 1998, p. 191.

5 God's gift to the world

1 I am indebted here to Clare Amos, who pointed out the significance of reconciliation in Genesis – see her 'The Genesis of Reconciliation: The Reconciliation of Genesis', *Mission Studies*, 23.1, Koninklijke, Brill, 2006.

2 *Choose to Love – Brother Roger of Taizé 1915–2005*, Taizé, Ateliers et Presses, 2006, p. 71.

3 M. Fidanzio, *Brother Roger of Taizé*, New York, Orbis, 2006, p. 21.

4 Fidanzio, *Brother Roger*, pp. 41, 62, 20.

5 D. Tutu, *No Future Without Forgiveness*, London, Rider, 1999, p. 221.

6 G. Daly, 'Forgiveness and Community', in A. Falconer and J. Liechty (eds), *Reconciling Memories*, Dublin, Columba Press, 1998, p. 214.

7 Quoted in John Allen, *Rabble-Rouser for Peace*, London, Rider, 2007, p. 341.

Select bibliography

Allen, John, *Rabble-Rouser for Peace*, London, Rider, 2007.

Amos, Clare, 'The Genesis of Reconciliation: The Reconciliation of Genesis', *Mission Studies*, 23.1, Koninklijke, Brill, 2006.

Arendt, H., *The Human Condition*, Chicago, University of Chicago Press, 1998.

Bayley, John, *Iris – A Memoir of Iris Murdoch*, London, Abacus, 1999.

Brueggemann, W., *Hopeful Imagination*, Philadelphia, Fortress Press, 1986.

Choose to Love – Brother Roger of Taizé 1915–2005, Taizé, Ateliers et Presses, 2006.

Cragg, K., *Palestine – The Prize and Price of Zion*, London, Cassell, 1997.

De Gruchy, John W., *Reconciliation – Restoring Justice*, London, SCM, 2002.

Falconer, A. and Liechty, J. (eds), *Reconciling Memories*, Dublin, Columba Press, 1998.

Fidanzio, M., *Brother Roger of Taizé*, New York, Orbis, 2006.

Mandela, Nelson, *Long Walk to Freedom*, Randburg, South Africa, Macdonald Purnell, 1994.

Muhyi al-Din Ibn al-Zaki, 9 October, 1187, quoted in Mariam Shahin, *Palestine – A Guide*, Massachusetts, Interlink, 2005.

Munayer, Salim J. (ed.), *In the Footsteps of our Father Abraham*, Jerusalem, Musalaha, 2002.

Rogers, Carl, *On Becoming a Person*, Boston, Houghton Mifflin, 1961.

Sachs, Jonathan, *The Dignity of Difference*, London, Continuum, 2002.

Schreiter, R., 'The Theology of Reconciliation and Peacemaking for Mission', in Mellor, H. and Yates, T. (eds), *Mission, Violence and Reconciliation*, Sheffield, Cliff College, 2004, pp. 11–28.

Tomkins, Stephen, *William Wilberforce – a Biography*, Oxford, Lion, 2007.

Tutu, D., *No Future Without Forgiveness*, London, Rider, 1999.

Volf, M., *Exclusion and Embrace*, Nashville, Abingdon Press, 1996.

Volf, M., *The End of Memory*, Grand Rapids, Eerdmans, 2006.

Williams, James G. (ed.), *The Girard Reader*, New York, Herder & Herder, 2004.

Yehoshua, A. B., *The Wall and the Mountain*, Tel-Aviv, Zemorah-Bitan, 1989.

Zizioulas, John D., *Communion and Otherness*, London, T&T Clark, 2006.